UNFOLDING SUCCESS

NEW ERA NEW APPROACH

A practical handbook that guarantees bringing happiness in your professional and personal life

SAPAN BARDHAN

First Edition: June 2019
Second Edition: September 2019
Third Edition: January 2021
Printed in India

Printed at Dhote Offset Printer, Mumbai
Typeset in Adobe Garamond Pro

ISBN: 978-93-88698-02-3

Cover Illustration: Prashant, Shyambesh and Team StoryMirror

STORYMIRROR
Stories that reflect you

Publisher:	StoryMirror Infotech Pvt. Ltd. 145, First Floor, Powai Plaza, Hiranandani Gardens, Powai, Mumbai - 400076, India

Web:	https://storymirror.com
Facebook:	https://facebook.com/storymirror
Twitter:	https://twitter.com/story_mirror
Instagram:	https://instagram.com/storymirror

Dedicated to

All Citizens of 'Bharat'

"The fragrance of flowers spread only in the direction of the wind, but Goodness of a Person spreads in all directions"

Sri Chanakya

Prologue

Chapters

Why this Book may Change Your Life!

What does success mean to you?

To some, success is wealth; for some, it is power; some just want to make a positive impact on the world.

This simply means that success is a concept that means different things to different people. No matter what success means to you, it almost certainly isn't something that will come easily.

There are numerous books in the market on how to be successful. But success is very personal and unique to each individual. Though some of these numerous books can be definitely useful to some readers, the advice contained in most of these books may often be very generic in nature, and at times, irrelevant to most of the readers.

With this in mind, before initiating the book, the author has taken a tremendous and sincere effort of talking to more than three hundred people, just to understand 'what exactly did they want from such a book? These candidates, both men and women, come from different age groups and different backgrounds - academics, economic, cultural and geographic backgrounds.

The author has effectively blended his own vast professional and social experience along with the inputs of all these three hundred people that he talked to. The author's own life journey has been full of ups and downs. So he could very well relate to the needs of the prospective readers.

Also, a word of caution - Success will not just come automatically simply by reading this book. But this book will definitely give you the necessary torch to find your way through the dark lanes of life.

There is no single right way to be successful. What works for you might not work for someone else. There may not be a perfect combination of ingredients that can guarantee success, but this book provides you with some basic steps which you can follow that can improve your chances of being successful in life, love, work, or whatever you feel ... are important to you!

Happy Reading!

Inspirations !!!

... Encouraging comments on the first edition of the book!

Acknowledge receipt of 'Unfolding Success'. Honorable Former President, Late Shri Pranab Mukherjee extends his good wishes for all your future endeavors!

Ms. Damini Kukreja 12th Aug'2019
Addl. Pvt. Secretary to Honorable Former President of India

Honorable Vice President of India has acknowledged with thanks, the book titled 'Unfolding Success'!

Shri D Prashanth K Reddy, IAS 25th July'2019
Pvt. Secretary to Vice-President of India

Acknowledge with thanks the letter addressed to the Honorable Prime Minister, along with a book titled 'Unfolding Success', written by you!

Shri Chandresh Sona 6th Dec'2019
Director - PMO's Office

Many thanks for your book 'Unfolding Success', looking forward to reading with great interest!

Shri Manmohan Singh 24th July'2019
Honorable Former Prime Minister, India

Received your first published book 'Unfolding Success'. Book contains interesting and useful information - Good Wishes for the grand success of the book!

Shri Amit Shah 13th Sept'2019
Honorable Home Minister

Thanks for the wonderful book 'Unfolding Success'. It's a fascinating book providing valuable and practical insights for happiness in a highly complex world.

I am sure the book will be a resounding success, wish you all happiness!

Shri Amitabh Kant — 24th July'2019

Honorable CEO – NITI Aayog

Received your letter and the book 'Unfolding Success'. I convey my hearty congratulations and wish continual improvement and progress in your creativity!

Shri Ramesh Pokhriyal 'Nishank' — 4th Sept'2019

Honorable Minister of HRD

In receipt of your first published book titled 'Unfolding Success', and thanks for the book.

I congratulate you for putting up your forty-two year's work experience in people – management, engagement and development. It is indeed very informative and covers various aspects in a very lucid, simple, and elaborate way!

Shri Prakash Javadekar — 29th July'2019

Honorable Minister of I & B

Author's Imagination of 'Bharat Beyond 2021'

'Books are the means by which we build bridges between cultures. Knowledge gives us power, love gives us fullness.'

Dr. Sarvepalli Radhakrishnan

From the Author's Desk

Greetings!

Our sincere salute to all those who have stepped up during current unprecedented times of the pandemic COVID-19, that has disrupted the world; to the Leadership of Central and all State Governments, Bureaucrats, Doctors and Para Medical Staff, entire Police Department and of course, the People on the ground, serving at our doorsteps every day, to meet our daily needs.

But the current pandemic situation across the world has also taught us many things. We now understand that our daily requirements are not much and that we can adapt to the new normal with lesser needs.

Our salute to all the brave soldiers and the entire military staff, safeguarding our loving country, round the clock on the borders in deserts in summer and at Himalayan mountains in the chilly winter, without worrying about their own lives, their own families and their children's future!

My professional and social life experiences spanning over forty-five years has made me realize that we may always aspire for the world to change to suit our requirements or wishes but the question is how far are we willing to change our thoughts, our actions, our comments on others, considering the consequence of their actions.

This new edition has been upgraded with new perspectives which will certainly help you to reflect on different aspects of life and pave the way for self-actualization. These tools will not only enable you in achieving results at workplaces but also help in filling you with a sense of inner peace and fulfillment … the ultimate success. A calm and cool mind is the foundation to create wonders and bring many laurels and feathers on your cap!

This book highlights the need to empower our citizens in the real sense, particularly women by encouraging compulsory education and medical facilities but to my personal opinion - distributing freebies may be limited as a policy except in extraordinary times such as natural calamities or the current pandemic. The reason is, it may make people lazy and as time passes they won't be able to support their families comfortably leading to unrest.

Everyone in the country must get busy with some work or the other and earn money so as to live with pride and dignity in the society. The overall objective should be to create an aura of positivity to influence people to think good, get engaged in improvement initiatives and contribute … to the organisation, society and thus ultimately to the nation's growth. It will come back to us, for sure! Age cannot be a hurdle, but with age effectiveness improves and so does efficiency; may not be physically but the years of rich experience silently directs him 'to focus only on value addition or prioritised activities' …

really those needed to be done. We see how the elderly leaders of the country are working hard with the sole objective of taking our country to the world level. The Government Authorities may think of utilising the expertise/services of willing senior citizens for creating positive vibes within societies - a need of the hour today - and initiate improvements by respecting their contribution through honorarium.

This may serve at least four purposes:–

i. engaging them results in creating a sense of value and pride within them.

ii. they would get busy with valuable work and therefore unlikely to waste time on unwanted issues.

iii. their expertise and rich long term experience will certainly add value to the society and nation as well, that too at insignificant costs.

iv. an improved environment of happiness is likely to prevail across the country or states wherever implemented. It is said that 'giving happiness to others brings back happiness to the giver'.

The New Education Policy is a great step towards building a Great Nation! It is education … education … and … only education which can bring out their hidden talents and motivate them to put forth newer ideas that are of crucial importance to the country today. The new policy has also focussed on skills development along with theoretical knowledge. This will help us to become truly 'आत्मनिर्भर भारत'. We need to focus not only on the youngsters but also on elderly people in a very big way across the country; no person as an individual is bad but they may lack basic value systems and get influenced by others who may not be aware of our highly valued cultural system. In the past we have seen that in case of any crisis ... all become ONE! ONE BHARAT! Irrespective of different languages, varied state cultures, different economic status, different political ideologies ... all become one! Great! In Hindi it is referred to as विविधता में एकता or अनेकता में एकता (Unity in Diversity) ... What a rich culture our ancestors have gifted us!

One thing must be kept in our mind that the Rashtra Dharma overrides all other existing dharmas. ... It exists, and therefore we exist!

When we talk about education, it should be the right kind of education that emphasizes not only on the job-fetching certificates but also on the basics of our country's culture, family systems, civic sense, our individual responsibilities towards family, society and nation ... otherwise in an unrest, why are vehicles/trains etc broken or burnt, whether national or personal properties ? These are direct losses to the nation and each of us suffers.

Yes, we need plenty of manufacturing, service and entertainment set-ups for people to get jobs or start own businesses and earn money for their own and fulfill family's genuine requirements. Once these areas are taken care, many of unwarranted issues are likely to drastically come down, because everyone would be engaged and busy with no time to think about nonsense activities.

I would also like to add one more area of concern in the country today i.e. increasing trend of population growth. It's the responsibility of one and all to think very seriously;

otherwise, it may become like a dragon that shall ruin all developmental efforts of the country. It's suggested that like New Education Policy, a Policy on 'Population Control' may also be formalized soon for effective implementation.

Let's hope the best days come from the year 2021 onwards.

We must remember what Bharat Ratna Shri J.R.D TATA Sir said:

"No success or achievement in material terms is worthwhile unless it serves the needs or interests of the country and its people and is achieved by fair and honest means"

Sometimes we come to know about disputes among certain very rich families having huge wealth created by the untiring and rigorous efforts of one or two individuals over many years but when the disputes start … where is peace in their minds? We need to really introspect!

Though the world today run by Information Technology because of which communication has become very fast across the world within no time, I personally feel that human touch is needed in these interactions. Toll-Free numbers of the automatic communication system are one of the examples.... very difficult to communicate real issues, long waiting time to talk to executives since they are busy with other important clients, electronic mails come with 'No Reply mode', a collective thought process of wiser employees may certainly avoid a high level of frustration among customers.

Similarly, it would be a good idea to have after-sale service cells within the same premises of sale points. It will not only ensure better quality of service but will also be a true homage to our Mahatma Gandhiji who used to say 'Customers ?

are God ? in your premises', and should not remain a mere display board .

In fact, this is the essence of Total Quality Management'.

Even after approximately 70 years of independence, people are dying due to repeated floods in some parts of the country where-as farmers are struggling to have seasonal crops on time, because of insufficient water to irrigate. Surprisingly, crops are ruined in absence of adequate storage facility too. I am sure officials concerned must be in the process of finding better solutions.

What we need today is strong leadership … leadership to motivate others … leadership of self-discipline… leadership by example.

The great cricketer Mr. Sourav Ganguly is an outstanding example how to motivate the members of the team at the risk of foregoing personal gains.

I watched him in a video, sharing his experience in a school at Kolkata. He mentioned that one's career cannot be a straight line; ups and downs will always be there. Sachin played approximately 700 innings and made 100 centuries. In 2003, he added - when India was to tour Australia - the selection committee more or less finalised two spinners. At that time another bowler 'Mr. A', though quite popular, was not performing well; but Sourav, knowing that he was one of the best spinners and if he was not selected then, might lose forever, conveyed to the committee that he also needed 'Mr. A' on the team. Since the committee was reluctant, Sourav told 'until you don't include him, I won't leave the meeting room'. Finally, the committee agreed but cautioned that if

Mr. A did not perform well, Sourav's own career might be impacted. Sourav agreed, and the rest is history.

Result: in the last test match of the series 'Mr. A' took the highest number of wickets and India won the test for the first time in Australia's ground.

This episode teaches us two lessons:

1. High level of confidence in 'Mr. A' placed by the leader
2. Leadership of the captain who risked his own career, in supporting a deserving player to regain his position.

Sourav rightly pointed out that all contestants in election sometimes fail; also, if a student fails in one semester does not mean that he won't perform better in the next! We all need to move past our failures.

Another example of self-discipline or self-control is our Captain Cool, Mr. Mahendra Singh Dhoni. It will be a hard task to find a person like him … talking only whenever really needed, no self praise, no loud voice, his body language never showing any signs of being a great cricketer or becoming rich starting from the ranks of a railway working staff.

Our salute to both the international cricketers who are the pride of Bharat!.

Our country needs these types of leaders who take care of others before self and we have Industrial Leaders like:

Shri Ratan Tata, Azim Premji, Narayan Murthy, Anand Mahindra, Cyrus Poonawalla, Sushil Goenka, Inder Jaisinghani and Brothers (Polycab Group), Rajiv Bajaj … to name a few among many.

According to Mother of Sri Aurobindo Ashram, we need 'Divine Management' in today's Corporate World.

Brahmakumari sister Sunita says we need to change ourselves first before changing the world, and the Divine God Father Shiva says 'the ones who, with an easy nature, constantly think of solutions instead of problems are free from the burden of problems. They constantly contribute to making things easy for themselves and for others too'.

We all need Peace around the World. Sister Shivani urges to make a habit of speaking high energy words and says in the current 'new normal' we need Emotional Fitness, in addition to physical fitness.

Dr. Alok Pandey of Sri Aurobindo Ashram says 'there must be someone who has created the universe' and adds, 'योगक्षेमं वहाम्यहम्' ... God is taking our responsibility.

I believe, everything is possible. Only we need to genuinely wish, plan and execute. If Israel can convert sea water into pure drinking water, why can't we? We have lots of intelligent people in our country; we only need to provide them resources and continue motivating them till desired results are achieved.

Lot of issues have accumulated over the years, thankfully the government is sorting out the issues one by one, on the basis of the nation's priorities and focusing more on bringing stability to the basic requirement of the country in the present scenario.

We must know who we are! All of us have great strengths of various types and in different fields; only we need to recognise our enormous capabilities and feel powerful within.

Somewhere, I read that happiness is like balloons … very difficult to find the one out of many which bears 'my name', but if we can pick up any one having somebody else's name written, and can pass it on to the respective person smilingly, that person would be happy. If the same policy is adopted by one and all, probably everyone will get the balloon with his own name within the quickest time possible.

We look for happiness and fight life - long to enjoy happiness like a deer who desperately runs in deserts in search of water but can't. Happiness is like 'मृगतृष्णा' in a desert of our materialistic world. It's said, "If we try to give happiness to others, the same will automatically come back to us" … It's law of attraction … so simple.

The super almighty always tells that if your intentions are good, clear and honest, many people will come to support you!

I am witnessing this!

The first edition of 'Unfolding Success', got very good response.

I take this opportunity to specially thank -

Honorable secretaries/office executives of:

Former President of India – Late Shri Pranab Mukherjee,

Vice President of India - Shri M. Venkaiah Naidu,

Prime Minister of India - Shri Narendra Modi,

Former Prime Minister of India – Shri Manmohan Singh,

Shri Amit Shah – Honorable Home Minister,

Shri Amitabh Kant – Honorable CEO, NITI Ayog,

Shri Ramesh Pokhriyal 'Nishank' – Honorable Minister of Education

Shri Prakash Javadekar – Honorable Minister of I & B

~ for their encouragement and good wishes to me!

The Success Factors!

Some of the dignitaries who responded well to our survey on 'SUCCESS Exercise' (prioritizing the parameters of success, what success means to them etc.) are:

Dr. Pratap Dighavkar, IPS - Special Inspector General of Police (P.C.W.C), Maharashtra;

Dr. Sudhakar Shinde, IRS - CEO, Ayushman Bharat, (MS);

Dr. Indrajit Bhattacharya - Director, NABET

(National Accreditation Board for Education & Training, Govt. of India)

Shri Rajesh Kumar Arnold, IES - Ex. Board Member of TRAI;

CA Vijay Singh Bapna - Past International President, Apex (2015 – 2019) Mahavir International

Shri Abhay Daptardar - Astt. Director, Ministry of MSME, Govt. of India;

Shri Ramesh T Jaisinghani - Director, Polycab India Ltd;

Shri Ganesh Deshmukh – Past Municipal Commissioner, Panvel, (MS)

Shri M G Arun - Executive Editor, India Today;

Shri Anurag Rastogi – Joint Director, NABET, QCI (Quality Council of India);

Dr. Radhakrishna Pillai - Best Seller Author, Dy. Director,

CIILS, University of Mumbai;

Our Sincere Thanks are also to following personalities for their contributions to this book:

Swami Satyadevananda - Secretary, Ramakrishna Mission, Mumbai;

CA Vijay Singh Bapna – Past International President (Apex) Mahavir International;

BK Usha Didi for delivering an excellent talk on Bhagavad Gita at Vile Parle, Mumbai in February'2020;

Dr. E V Swaminathan - Brahmakumari's Vidyalaya, Mount Abu;

Shri Manoj Das Gupta – Managing Trustee, Sri Aurobindo Ashram, Pondicherry for guiding me to write on 'Sri Aurobindo International Centre of Education'.

Shri Ajay & Ramesh Jaisinghani – the Directors of Polycab India, for their inspirational journey of 'Connecting with aspirations'.

Shri Rajendra Potdar – CEO, MABEC for writing another real success story on 'Lean Manufacturing at MSME Clusters, Aurangabad', where I myself was involved for execution.

Purpose of including write ups from above Spiritual and Social Organisations is to make people more aware of their excellent efforts for bringing a positive change within the society and the practical experiences of the persons involved with industries to inspire others willing to excel in their respective fields.

Shri Shrikrishna Patankar, a brilliant artist to sketch down my thoughts of 'Bharat Beyond 2021 …'.

Shri V V Jamnis, Mahim Jain, D S Chandrashekhar, Dilip Jha, Rajendra Potdar and Dr. (Smt.) Rama Bhosle and many others for their candid and encouraging feedback on the Book.

Shri Bibhu Raut – CEO, Story Mirror and his dedicated team for supporting enthusiastically in getting the 'New Edition published'.

and of course to our Editorial Team comprising of professional experts M/s Atul Kulkarni, Harshal Pradhan and Reval Hejmady.

All of us know many of top posts globally are occupied by the people of our country … CEOs, Scientists, Doctors, IT Experts, R & D and so on.

Within our own country quite a few may not be very happy, get disappointed frequently; but one thing is for sure - that we all are very much safe, may meet families and friends, enjoy celebrations but what about others who are on the borders who are not sure of tomorrow, their family members keep waiting for their loved ones!!! But in spite of all these, their confidence continues.

I conclude with two meaningful stories:

During a local football match, when a person enquired with one of the team's supporters 'What's the result now?'

The supporter replied with a smile that the opposite team is leading by 3-0. The person further asked 'But how come you are not looking discouraged?' The supporter replied 'Why should I? The referee has not yet blown the final whistle. I am confident that my team will win'. Finally, the supporter's team won by 5-4. What a level of confidence!

But what is the general scenario; we get frustrated and start whistling within? In fact our responsibility is to focus on what we are supposed to do within a defined period without worrying about the whistle.

So, the games are still on and let's hope for a better result.

One fine morning school-going children complained to a monk that a snake around a tree always chases them and tries to bite. The monk while passing by the tree asked the snake why he made them afraid, he should not be doing so. The snake agreed. After few days again the monk was passing by the tree and found the snake injured and heavily bleeding and seriously injured. The monk felt very sad about the snake. He was worried and asked the snake – how did it happen, who made his condition so bad?

The snake replied him about those children and how every time they pass by, they start stoning on it. On asking why it did not object, snake replied that since it had promised him not to try harming them it did not scare them off. The monk remembered the incident and with sympathy told that he had asked not to bite or harm them but never told 'that you go on tolerating their inhuman actions and don't even express your anger by raising your head up and make them afraid of you'! A lesson for all of us and the country too. Our culture says to have cordial relations with everybody, but now times have changed.

Future of our country, BHARAT, is expected to be very bright beyond the year 2021; provided we all together as a team support the various initiatives of the government. We have to win and would certainly win to showcase the greatness of our country to the rest of the world … no going back … if not for us, let's worry and work for the new generations to come hereafter and gift them a life of comfort, pride and dignity!

The time has come to look within and question ourselves, whether our deeds so far were right or wrong and accordingly either continue to be happy, or act to prevent recurrence of those wrong acts in future forever. Every act of ours should be based on inner consciousness and for the benefits of people at large especially the underprivileged. Out of the learnings we are having recently, better to expect a better governance system like of 'Ram Rajya' based on truth, non-violence and moral principles, not only within our country but across the world … sooner the better!

Let's together create an 'Environment of Love with 'Zero Tolerance of Hatred' and keeping 'Rashtra Dharma' on top of our all dharmas, as because only if the nation exists, we exist.

Sincerely yours and with Best Regards,

Sapan Bardhan **16th October'2020**
New Panvel, Navi Mumbai (MS)

DECLARATION

The objective of the book is to make students, entrepreneurs, professionals and employees at different levels - aware of the issues/hurdles that are normally present in most of organizations and the skill to tackle them using techniques, which are difficult to be taught in schools and colleges for practical reasons. This book aims to support every citizen of the country to excel in their own work and thus help them in adding greater value to their own businesses, the organizations where they are employed, besides improving the economic status of all involved and contributing to the growth of the nation and to be a **successful and happy person**.

DISCLAIMER:

The author might have cited many unpleasant situations/ issues faced by him that were creating a barrier to his own as well as the organization's growth. He does not have any intention to hurt anyone's sentiments. Resemblance to any part of the book with anybody's working or personal life may be simply a coincidence!

Foreword

I met Sapan for the first time when he came to attend my workshop on 'How to write a book and make it a bestseller". He was already determined that his book will be published soon. His commitment to writing a book was contagious. A lot of people show initial enthusiasm, but later with time, it dies off. I am glad that finally the book is out and in your hands.

Sapan has written the book in a nice and creative way. It will inspire many others to become successful in life. The book is like a road map that will help you in every stage of your life. You, as readers, will surely connect with the book right from the beginning. Sapan's writing style is simple, yet profound.

Dr. Radhakrishnan Pillai
Deputy Director,
Chanakya International Institute of Leadership Studies (CIILS)
University of Mumbai
Author (8 Best sellers) - Corporate Chanakya / Chanakya's 7 secrets of leadership / Chanakya in You / Katha Chanakya / Chanakya in daily life / Inside Chanakya's mind - Aanvikshiki and the art of thinking / Thus spoke Chanakya / Chatur Chanakya and the Himalayan problem (Best selling children's book)

Chapter 1

Interpreting Success

India has always enjoyed an edge over its counterparts whenever a comparison has been drawn on the lines of cultural heritage and its richness. Our country often referred to as 'The Golden Bird' (Sone ki Chidiya) has since ages attracted visionaries to missionaries and traders to invaders, to come and explore this magical land to fulfil their respective vision and mission. As time passed by, the status of richness started to dwindle and fade away, a heartfelt truth which we are all aware of. But simultaneously, we also see some silver lining along the dark clouds as we have started to witness the indices of economic growth and development grow slowly, but in an upward trend that is favourable to all of us. It is thus evident that the same resources and abilities of a nation with the right type of leadership could motivate us to ensure that the future of all our countrymen is bright.

There is hardly anyone on this planet who does not wish to succeed and be regarded as successful. But as we all start our hunt for success, the question that crops up is where does the buck stop ? According to me, the yardstick for measuring success is not the wealth that one has earned over his/her lifetime. Success in its true sense is fostering an essence of all-round achievement. In other words, it is the ability to be holistically successful. I echo verbatim the words of a learned soul who has described success saying, 'As we try and reach out for our goals and milestones, we ought to remain light and keep our actions positive thereby ensuring that we move in the right direction.

This will ensure our happiness and this in fact is true success.'

We find ourselves struggling day in and day out in search of happiness. We are yet to realize the very simple but significant fact that being happy depends on ourselves. Success is to experience and feel the essence of achievement at every step, and not just feel it when we are on the verge of reaching our destination. As an individual, we need to gauge our inner strength; in short, the capability within ourselves that echoes our commitment, 'Yes, I made it happen'. A professional speaker has proclaimed that once a person has reached the top of an organization, no excuses can be accepted for not being able to achieve success. This is a harsh truth because one must have already been successful enough to climb to one of the top positions of any organization.

Henry Ford, Thomas Alva Edison, Dhirubhai Ambani, Steve Jobs and Inder Jaisinghani have all been very successful in their endeavours, even though none of them had very high level of academic qualification. The success stories of differently-abled personalities like Sudha Chandran, Arunima Sinha need no citation. Abraham Lincoln and Franklin Roosevelt had failed many times, but they were confident in their abilities and continued their journey to become the President of USA. N R Narayana Murthy, Lata Mangeshkar, A. R. Rehman, APJ Abdul Kalam, Narendra Modi, Rajnikant, Keshu Bhai Patel and Dhirubhai Ambani achieved success despite their financial challenges. While Sachin Tendulkar and Aamir Khan fell short in their physical height, Adnan Sami had excess of body weight; but nothing stopped them to kiss stardom in their respective fields. Colonel Harland Sanders, the Founder of KFC, an American fast-food chain became a popular businessman only after attaining 60 years of age. Swapna Barman, the daughter of a rickshaw puller, has recently done our country proud by bagging a gold medal at the Jakarta Asian Games. Google, Microsoft, Amazon, Apple and HP, to name a few of the renowned companies, were ones that started off from a garage, as I am told.

We also know by now how Remo D'Souza and Kapil Sharma have struggled in their lives before making their positions in their respective areas of entertainment, i.e. dance and stand-up comedy.

So, where does the problem lie for us ? Our problem lies in the fact that we lack in setting a long-term vision and mission for our life. We lack a strong will to achieve something extraordinary. We need to realize our true potential in order to achieve success. We also need to identify our weaknesses so that we can selectively discard the bad qualities in ourselves and start marching towards our defined goal. Success truly depends on determination, faith, and hard work.

I am aware that the question that is bothering your mind now is, 'HOW DO I MAKE IT ?' For an insight into this query, please go through the remaining chapters with the right spirit. You will discover ways to develop your strategy and plan out your execution with the right tools to seek your goal, as foreseen by you in your vision.

Life is like driving a vehicle

One of the comparisons which help in self-realization is that while driving a vehicle the driver represents the spiritual energy, and the car represents the body. Body is controlled by the spiritual energy. The biggest reason why I do not have the desired control over my physical body, my vehicle, and my sense organs today is that I have lost the consciousness of being a driver who could control and rule the vehicle. Instead, I have developed the consciousness that I am this vehicle, this physical body. This consciousness disconnected me from the ability and the power I possessed inside me to control the vehicle.

If I want to achieve the desired control, I need to be in a mode of driver-consciousness i.e.

I am a soul and my body is a vehicle through which I experience life.

The car controls are the gears, brakes, accelerator and steering wheel which can be compared to the sense organs of the soul such as the mind, intellect and sanskaras and those of the body which are the eyes, ears, nose, hands and tongue. A good driver is one who remains extremely alert and can use the gears, brakes, accelerator and steering wheel effectively and efficiently, in order to be fully in control of the vehicle and avoid any accidents. In the same way, as I move on the road of life, I need to keep my mental and physical sense organs in complete control. If I do that, these sense organs will keep my journey enjoyable and take me to my desired destination of mental peace and happiness, safely and successfully.

If I don't do that and let them overpower me, accidents will occur, i.e. absence of peace and a sorrowful life will be the destination reached.

If a good driver, while driving a car is distracted by the negative and disturbing scenario that he comes across and his attention is pulled in many different directions, he will make his journey unsafe, increasing the probability of meeting with accidents. When the same principles are applied to the soul and the body, I also need to take care that, while travelling on the road of life, I am not distracted by scenes that are not useful to me. Example, when looking out through my eyes and I don't have to take in all the images, scenes and information along the way, otherwise I may meet with an accident. When listening through my ears, I don't have to take in all the words and everything that people say; otherwise I may meet with an accident. I can choose to absorb only what is useful for me, but I do not have to register distracting, negative and harmful images and words. Just like a driver, I see and understand situations; I also keep my eyes and ears open - it would be unsafe to ignore them completely, I need to be aware of them - but I look only for the positive in them, so that I remain focused and am not deflected from my goal of experiencing inner contentment and bliss, while making the journey.

Key Take Away:

We, as the driver in charge of this vehicle - the body, also need to take care that we do not drive rashly i.e. learn to monitor the feelings and attitude that is transmitted outwards through our eyes, our words, and our complete body language. Driving rashly

I.e. transmitting negative energy in this way could harm any co-traveller on the road of life. When these feelings stay positive, filled with sweetness, purity and respect, it helps to ensure that our journey is smooth and enjoyable. When we stay alert and aware in driver-consciousness and drive carefully, our actions bring us closer to our spiritual truth and we can share our positivity with others around us. When we lose awareness for even a moment, there's a danger either from you to others, or vice versa.

Chapter 2

What Success means to Them!

Responses from Prominent Personalities of the Society

What 'Success' means to leaders holding various key positions, i.e. bureaucrats, heads of important industries, educational institutions, hospitals and media, authors, consultants, and others.

The questionnaire given below was circulated to prominent personalities with a request to respond:

A. What does success mean to you?

B. How do you rate your level of success at professional and Personal fronts, on a scale of 1 to 3 ?
3: Highly Successful; 2: Successful; 1: Not so successful

C. What are personal qualities and management style that you feel are responsible for your success?

D. Please rank and prioritise the following attributes/qualities based on your experiences needed in becoming successful:

1. Hard work
2. Passion
3. Compassion
4. Focussed
5. Sincerity
6. Keeping updated with latest management tools and techniques
7. Walk the talk
8. Mutual trust
9. Time Management

10. Work life balance

11. Social

12. Any other

E. Tell us about your significant achievements and how you met those.

F. How your profession is linked to the betterment of our society and nation?

G. Do you feel the vision and mission for every organisation and individual must be to embrace success?

H. What are your comments on the following?
   a. People management
   b. Motivational initiatives
   c. Learning – Un-learning – Re-learning

I. How important it is to be responsible and disciplined by one and all towards safety (on the road - safe driving and obey traffic rules, and safe practices within and outside of organisation), helping attitude towards senior citizens, police department, taking care of domestic animals, etc.)

J. Your specific message to the younger generation – the future leader of our country - to contribute in a better way.

K. Any other points, you may like me to convey to the country, during my forthcoming training/workshop programmes.

The answers/views as received are analysed and shared below for better understanding of different views. Out of the 37 people who were requested to fill up the questionnaire, 95% of them have responded.

X. What does success mean to you?

Some meaningful and interesting responses are cited below.

'Happiness by growth and achievements, along with letting others grow with you and making people's livelihood by creating employment.'

'Success means continually moving towards excellence and fulfilment.'

'Success means to achieve the essence of something that you set out to do for the greater happiness of people around you.'

'Being happy and keeping my family happy.' 'To have inner satisfaction and be happy.'

'Achieving the career objectives, I have set for myself.'

'Success means contentment to me; a realization that I have achieved a goal with satisfaction to its fullest.'

'Success is achieving goal/objective as per our plan or achieving something which makes me happy'.

Success means to have a goal, plan to achieve the goal, implement the plan, and finally achieve the goal. In other words, Success means to achieve a goal which I have set for myself.'

'Success means to produce high quality work before the target date.'

'Happiness of achieving goals.'

'Success to me is that progressive transformation one brings in personal, professional and societal aspects, leading to ultimate happiness.'

'Success had different connotations under different stages of my life. Formally/informally, I had set goals for me at different stages of my life and achieving those goals meant success to me. For example, as a sportsman I had set a target for myself to play at the University level. When I achieved it, I hung my boots and focused on something else in my life. As a student, I have set a target to acquire doctorate and I am quite close to it. As a professional I wanted that the organization which hires me must value my knowledge, experience and leadership, the valuation can be in terms of position/role/ remuneration etc'.

'Achieving more than 90% of everything you plan at professional level and personal level'

'Accomplishment, self-satisfaction, marching forward with target fulfilment.'

'It's a journey, a journey of transformation that you experience while you grow as a person.

It's a journey of feeling satisfied while you transformed the society around you. It's a journey of feeling responsible while you contribute your part in Nation Building. It's a journey of constantly becoming which never ends.'

'I think a clear distinction has to be made between material success and success that comes with activities of the mind, including better knowledge, wisdom, humanity, empathy for others (both humans and animals), and an understanding of the larger realities of life.

A truly successful person, according to me, is one who is able to balance his successes in the material world – a fulfilling job, career, business or any other profession, and good health

- with intellectual and spiritual pursuits (by 'spiritual' I mean an elevated thought that comes with a broad realisation of life and its transience, and a deep empathy for others, rather than any religious pursuit)'.

'Success is the result of activity performed consistently till you succeed.'

'Success to me is that which brings me joy and happiness. It could be helping someone who is in need or a job accomplished the desired way or a better way. Those everyday events that bring me joy is success.'

'Having purpose for living & loving and giving our best for the purpose'

Y. The Analysis:

A. How do you rate your level of success at Professional and Personal fronts, in a scale of 1 to 3:

3: Highly Successful, 2: Successful, 1: Not so successful

Highly Successful: 22%
Successful: 78%

To the best of my knowledge all the eleven persons categorized themselves as being highly successful. Their personal qualities have been mentioned in the next part.

B. What are the personal qualities and management styles you feel are responsible for your success?

Dr. Pratap Dighavkar (IPS)
His motivational talk on the platform of Josh (Marathi), available on 'YouTube' is worth watching/ listening.

V S Bapna
Try to be calm and never come into stress
Lead the team from the front nurturing a team spirit
Always try to see ahead; be a visionary

Dr. Lakshmi Mohan
Perseverance; Grit and determination; Positive approach; Participative management; Assertive

Arvind Bodhankar
Knowledge; *Diverse experience; Leadership skills*

Anand Rao
Adaptability to any situation;
Empathy; Patience;
The Management style:

Clarity of role, motivating people with a pat on their back for a good job done, Encouraging Openness, Respect and dignity among team members

Rajesh Kumar Arnold
Sincerity; Devotion; Balance between work and life

Dr. Radhakrishnan Pillai
Time management; Networking; Team building;
Understanding human needs and aspirations;
Research ability and strategic thinking;
Spiritual foundation

Dr. Sudhakar Shinde
Honesty; Hard work; Sincerity; Team spirit

Siraz Henry
Team Work
Give Full freedom to people to demonstrate their talent
Not much pushy but get the work done as per my needs

C. **Please rank/prioritise the following attributes/qualities based on your experiences needed in becoming most successful:**

1. Hard work
2. Passion
3. Compassion
4. Focused
5. Sincerity
6. Keeping updated with latest management tools & techniques
7. Walk the talk
8. Mutual trust
9. Time Management
10. Work life balance
11. Social

The ranking of qualities as personal success factors of all the respondents are shown below:

Dr. Pratap Dighavkar (IPS)'s motivational talk on the platform of Josh (Marathi), available on 'YouTube' is worth watching/ listening.

According to Sri Ramesh Jaisinghani, the Director – Polycab Group, vision is a must for everyone desiring to excel and wish to do something great in their lives.

Dr. (Mrs.) Lakshmi Mohan, Director – ITM, Navi Mumbai is of the opinion that one should be ready to accept challenges.

Sri M G Arun, Chief Executive Editor – India Today, is confident in saying that there is no substitute to hard work but needs to be complemented with compassion and a sense of direction

Sri Satish Kalokhe, President – QCFI says 'Failure is not a crime, but a low aim is'.

It reminds me of what Nakajima San, the founder guru of TPM said, "Machines should be so designed that these become incapable of producing defective products".

Sri Rajesh Mishra, General Manager – Greaves Cotton Ltd. gives importance to day-to-day discipline and ability to think strategically.

Sri D K Srivastava, Executive Director - QCFI says 'Qualities and interest, and their priorities differ in every individual's life. Thus, it is indeed important to know themselves, to adapt the qualities before they adapt them because someone successfully adapted them for their success. What may work for one, may not work for the other. Thus, self-evaluation is important to grow in life'.

Dr. (Mrs.) Rama A. Bhosle, Principal – Govt College of Education, Panvel gives importance to decision making.

Dr. Sudhakar Shinde, CEO – Ayushman Bharat – gives importance to improvisation also.

Sri V S Bapna is working on 'LOVE ALL SERVE ALL'.

Sri Siraz Henry is very much focussed on his work. He gives importance to time management; doesn't want to waste time, neither money. He has directed nine films so far.

D. Tell us your significant achievements and how could you meet those

All the respondents shared their significant achievements which get validated by the qualities they possess.

E. How your profession is linked to the betterment of our society and nation

F. Do you feel vision and mission for every organisation and individual must be to embrace success?

Everyone said 'YES' as a key ingredient for success.

So, it's necessary for anyone who wants to taste success and enjoy its benefits to define their long term as well as short term dreams and draw up a relevant action plan to work accordingly.

G. What are your comments on the following?

a. **People management**
b. **Motivational initiatives**
c. **Learning – Un-learning – Re-learning**

All correspondents felt that this process is an integral part of management and have their own unique style of people management; but all of them have common opinion that motivation is needed for better results and Learning – Un-learning – Re-learning must be a continuous process.

H. How important is it to be responsible and disciplined by one and all towards – Safety (on the road - safe driving and obey traffic rules and safe practices within and outside of organisation), helping attitude towards Senior Citizens, Police department, looking at domestic animals sympathetically etc.

I. Your specific message to the younger generation – the future leader of our country to contribute in a better way

To learn from others in addition to your current knowledge and skills, continually upgrade, practice by self and by demonstrating to others your Leadership by example.

J. Any other points, you may like me to convey across the country, during my forthcoming training/workshop programmes.

Whatever is written in the book.

Chapter 3

Are you stuck in your Professional Journey?

The first and the foremost thing that one needs to remember and maybe more at times of despair is NOT TO GIVE UP! I would urge you to NOT LOSE HOPE. I quote the lines from a famous Hollywood movie, The Shawshank Redemption, 'Hope is a good thing, maybe the best of things and no good thing ever dies. Get busy living or get busy dying.

People usually get stuck up because they have not done or accomplished the following:

1. **Realistic and Proper Planning**

   Proper planning needs good homework and it starts with the question 'what am I supposed to deliver?' Answer(s) would be the tasks to perform. This should be followed by the next question 'By when?' Many a time, we just agree with the time frame without looking into the quantum of tasks to be completed. The answer to 'By when' is supposed to work as a base for resource planning. You must have read or heard somewhere that for success we need the 'right person with right skills for the right work'. Once the 'right work' is clear to you, both quantitatively and qualitatively, ask yourself whether the work is right for you. In other words, is this your cup of tea? If not, please try to avoid the work, which will otherwise become a headache for you causing depression in you. And do not forget that proper planning means day-wise planning.

2. **Adequate Skill Sets**

   All jobs need certain capabilities to perform. Look at your own capabilities and ask yourself if your capabilities are enough to perform the job. If yes, then don't worry. If not, find the gaps and upgrade yourself practically with the help of your known people. There is neither harm, nor shame in asking for help or support from your colleagues to get your job right. Nobody is perfect in all the games. They must have also sought help from their own colleagues at some point. There are people waiting to help you because the Almighty wants them to help you as an answer to your sincerity and honesty towards work.

3. **Self Confidence**

   Please revisit Chapter 1 of this book and ask yourself repeatedly 'If they can, why can't I?' Remember there is nobody in the world to stop you from succeeding. However, one must note that winning takes time. If you refer to chapter 1 again, you will realize that for everyone whosoever has reached their level of glory, it took them lot of time and perseverance, and they didn't leave halfway.

   'In which house I am born is not in my control, but in my birth what I am going to do is in my control.'

   - Chhatrapati Shivaji Maharaj

Late Mr. Subrato Basu was an employee of Bhilai Steel Plant who was passionate about acting and drama, and had won several awards in various competitions. He shifted his base to Mumbai around the 1990s for exploring opportunities in the film industry. Today everybody recognizes his son, Anurag Basu, as one of the popular film directors. Once in a show, Bollywood's actor Shah Rukh Khan once showed a photograph of an unnoticed boy lying on a floor. He went on to reveal that the boy was none other than the famous choreographer, Remo D'Souza. Remo took 21 years to finally choreograph in a movie starred by Shah Rukh Khan.

This is the journey of time. So, continue with your efforts sincerely and one day result will come. I am a firm believer of this quote by Swami Vivekananda and have realized it in my life too:

'If the mind is intensely eager, everything can be accomplished – mountain can be crumbled into atoms.'

There may be a gap in the time frame, but accomplishment is guaranteed. We have witnessed many matches that have been won with a dying minute goal or a last-ball six. These instances remind us that we need to keep trying till the lapse of our defined timelines.

So, please don't give up and do not lose hope. Remember that your family, our society and our country needs miracles from us. So, please do not get disappointed. We all believe 'you can and certainly you can because you are born to succeed'.

'Many of life's failures are people who did not realize how close they were to success when they gave up'

- Thomas Edison

Key Take Away

The road to success is never a straight one. Nor is it ever a single road that one must cross. Like a good cup of tea, success requires different things to be put together in right proportions. Ups, downs, faith, beliefs, sincerity, honesty, practicality, humility and courage

- when all these come together in the right way, success is difficult to miss.

Chapter 4

Strategies for Success!

Follow SQDCPEM or Safety, Quality, Delivery, Cost, Productivity, Environment, Morale, in a very disciplined and innovative way.

We have discussed that hard work and perseverance is must to get superior result; so believe in yourself and truly hope for a better result … after putting your best possible efforts …. also request almighty to help you and see the magic.

S: Safety

Safety aspects either on road, at home, or in the industries are not being given due importance as it should have been. Statistics show an increasing trend in accidents. You must have observed all vehicles, light or heavy, are found either on the zebra mark or even have crossed, at the time of facing red light/stop signals. Sometimes vehicles even cross when the signals are red. What is the hurry ? Unfortunately, it happens on all the four/five sides of crossings and then we blame the traffic police! Their job is to help us in ensuring safety rules, but the responsibility lies with us. Another unfortunate thing in case of any accident is that a lot of people gather from here and there. Some stand without extending a helping hand; others get busy in making a video of the incident, and yet others wait for the police to come. And most often than not, it gets too late to salvage anything by the time help arrives. Of course, a few come ahead, however less in number, to help. I salute them!

Thanks to Sachin Tendulkar who I heard of highlighting the necessity of giving passage to ambulances to move in emergencies. Thank you, Sachin, for stepping up to your responsibility as an MP and taking it up with the appropriate authorities. At this age, many a times I would get down from the vehicle and shout at the driver blocking the road. Surprisingly, I found them laughing at me!

Such is the also case in organizations, especially the unorganized ones. Safety gets a low priority and in some cases, there is no talk about safety at all! But in many multinationals, they have stringent guidelines to be followed by senior executives, and by themselves. The rest automatically follows. I have even heard that in case of any fatality, the head of the factory either gets suspended or yearly increments get stopped. Simply, aiming to establishing a system of ensuring zero accident/ incident is crucial.

I have myself witnessed a complete reversal of incidents since the time directors started keeping safety on top of the agenda during monthly progress reviews. Just shouting to express displeasure to the heads in case of any mishap and at the same appreciating and rewarding the combined efforts could lead to zero accidents.

Despite many hoardings and advertisements to wear helmets how many follow the rules? It's frequently common to see helmets kept on the handles than worn by the biker.

I urge all of you to think calmly for a while. We are not so rich a country. Many of us may be the only earning person in the family and taking care of old parents. If something happens to you either because of your own mistake or by others, what would happen to this family? When caused by others, the police will act, but what about the person who gets affected? How can we restore normalcy in their lives? Let us think together, let us follow this ideal first, and then ask others to follow. If people don't listen to you, don't worry; you have done your duty, but don't give up on following it yourself. One day people will follow you, too.

Let us all remember that an accident is caused and does not happen on its own; safety of self and others cannot and should not be compromised even at the cost of everything else. It is non-negotiable.

Safety in current situation:

I am confident, by now everyone is fully aware of what precautions to be taken in current pandemic environment - for self and others too like let's not move out unless and until really needed. But whenever we go out must wear appropriate masks to fully cover our mouth and nose. It would be better if hand gloves are used in case of going to offices, shops or any other public places etc., ensure use of a sanitizer as and when needed and once back home after a short trip, hands are adequately washed with soaps and preferably take a bath and the clothes are properly washed too.

People First!

Customer – Employee - Supplier are people-based; people is the only resource which gives output more than proportionate to input.

The customer and his requirement are always of prime significance. However, we should always bear in mind the thought of 'people first'. It is the people who can make goods, services and their experience either good or bad for the customers. They are the key players who will either fetch customer satisfaction or dissatisfaction. We must respect the workforce and maintain their dignity since it is their right to be treated with respect, dignity and fairness.

We should try and follow the popular saying 'praise in open but criticize in private'. Let us constantly question our conduct and look for areas of improvement within ourselves.

It is a universal truth and maybe something that must be strictly and diligently followed in India. Our families are big in number and the ratio of dependents to earners is quite high. So, we need to make our people constantly feel and realize what would happen if something untoward crops up with the family's earner? The entire family, majority of whom may be dependents, will lose their source of sustenance, and in the worst circumstances be forced to adopt a wrong path to meet their needs. Hence, whether we are at our workplace or on roads outside, we need to constantly keep in mind the safety of ourselves and others. In fact, let us adopt a zero-tolerance policy for ourselves for non-compliance to safety.

We have discussed on safety; now let us come to people management. You may find slogan written within the campus of many organizations as 'customer first'. It's correct, but who all would be taking care of customers? It's the people of the organization. Entrepreneurs of all cultured and profit-making organizations focus only on people. Their people management is so strong that they need not interfere in the day-to-day activities. Top management takes care of their own people like a family who in turn they take care of the customers very well. Bagging repeat business may not be a difficult task for them since all the three heads – supplier, organization and customers – work like the interconnected links of a strong chain for mutual benefits.

According to ***Richard Branson -***

Clients do not come first. Employees come first. If you take care of your employees, they will take care of your clients. Train people well enough so they can leave, treat them well enough so they don't want to.

Q: Quality

With quality normally we consider quality of products, but it's not just that. Quality is needed in everything we do daily - considering the requirements at family, of society, in the organizations by the bosses as well as subordinates, customer of products or services, and other - because the days are changing. Our environment is changing, customer requirements are changing, and it requires lot of effort to be in today's competitive world. Quality according to me is 'Zero Defect' in quality and in numbers. Zero defect is possible but requires a winning spirit. Days of 'Chalta Hai' are gone.

D: Delivery

Like quality, on time delivery, in TQM language Just in Time (JIT), is of utmost importance today. Your meals are needed when you are hungry. You must have heard of the incident where in a hospital many people suffered because of non-availability of oxygen cylinders. In a statement released after the incident, the higher officers said that they ordered the cylinders, but they were not supplied on time. The concerned people must have been punished, but can those children be brought back? Where is our value system going? Our country is known for its stress on values, but what's happening today will hardly keep up this reputation. And why this is happening must be answered by all of us together; and preventive measures must be made in place.

C: Cost

Old concept was

Expenses + Profit = Price, left side of the equation was solely decided by manufacturer

Current concept is

Price – profit = Expenses, where the left side is not in manufacturers' hand

He must manage the right side but must not be compromised at the cost of quality. Earning a good margin is possible, if we take care of the wastes we generate, non-value-adding activities we perform, utilizing maximum working time, making minimum number of meetings, that too for a short time, with a prefixed agenda.

I have seen in my career where many seniors feel that conducting a meeting is their responsibility.

Others are responsible for P, Q, C, and D

P: Productivity

The moment we start discouraging defective products or services, productivity automatically rises. The same is applicable to our daily activities also. Similarly, we may focus on getting rid of non-value adding processes and activities to increase productivity. The objective must be 'doing many activities together' and shortening the time taken simultaneously.

E: Environment

Two types of environment, I am talking about. One is the cleanliness and the level of pollution in and around. Thanks to all involved in government's cleanliness drive 'Swachhata Abhiyan' across the country. Though the speed is slow, but improvements of cleanliness can be seen at many locations. Second, the conduciveness in management style, free flow of information, everyone trying to do their best, accepting a mistake if committed openly, appreciation in open and criticism within closed doors. Self-esteem of all, especially at the bottom level, is needed to be kept high.

The above supports in enhancing moral of every human.

M: Moral and Morale

To my understanding, moral means the principles of right or wrong behaviour. As an individual we should have our own principles, either inherited from childhood or learnt from our parents, from the texts we read in schools or from great personalities and the good deeds they have done for the society and nation. We must be able to take a judgement of what is right or what is wrong for us, for the society, for any organization, and even for the nation in the long run.

Morale, on the other hand, means self- confidence and enthusiasm. Innovative ideas, improvement initiatives often come from the people having high a level of confidence and enthusiasm. Self-motivated people are less in numbers and hence it's the responsibility of the heads of family, organization and society's leaders to keep motivating people to a great extent, whenever and wherever possible.

Both moral and morale help build a culture of commitment. When inculcated into the culture, the level of both the 'M's, and safe practices can easily be sensed the way the security staff receives you at the gate, takes or directs you to a particular location.

Earning Money along with Blessings

Earning money is important as all types of physical comfort are bought with that money. However, money is not only a currency, it is also energy. It is loaded with invisible energy of how we earned it, which includes our intentions, thoughts, beliefs, behaviours, principles and ethics. If this energy is pure and positive, we bring home not just money but also the energies of peace, happiness and love. When such money with its pure energy is used to fulfil our family's needs and comforts, everyone's well-being is assured. Money earned ethically comes home with blessings, as it comes home after giving peace and happiness to others.

Let us be honest, clean and authentic in our thoughts and words. Let us co-operate with people, live our values and earn blessings of everyone working with us. Our money earned should not have a trace of any one's pain, dissatisfaction or discomfort. Create your own principles and ethics of the ways to earn and don't compromise on them.

Every morning, let us remind ourselves that we all are pure beings. We have to be sincere and honest in everything we do, carrying pure energy at our workplaces. Our thoughts, words and behaviours may earn us blessings the whole day, be at home or at work. Have beautiful professional relationships. Understand that to be successful you need to earn blessings along with earning money, need to complete tasks on time with efficiency and co-operate with everyone. Blessings given means Blessings earned. We all need to create positive vibes of happiness all around.

Key Take Away

We all are learners always ~

Setting a personal goal ~

Managing time and attention ~

Reviewing own performance ~

Work out a plan of any assignment ASAP ~

Anticipate problems ahead of execution ~

Discuss within the team and with the Boss whenever needed ~

Chapter 5
My Thoughts Create My Destiny

Spiritual wisdom teaches us that happiness is independent of our accomplishments, possessions and relationships. Yet, on some days we are happy, and on some days anxious. Some days we are enthusiastic and some days dull. This means that sometimes our feelings are not in our control. The fact is, each of us can create feelings and destiny of our choice using thought power. How do thoughts manifest destiny? Answer is in a simple chain moving forward sequentially from our thoughts to feelings, attitude, actions, habits, personality and destiny. Let us understand how they work.

1. My Every Thought Generates My Feeling. Thoughts are my creation. Every thought gives rise to a feeling; so how I feel is decided by the quality of my thought. If I consciously create a pure, positive thought, I will feel happy. Happiness is a feeling, an emotion and an experience I go through. Likewise, I also experience feelings like peace, love, pain, anger and others. Suppose I create a thought - I enjoy working in this office - it generates a positive emotion and I feel happy. On the contrary, if I create a thought - I dislike working here - it generates a negative emotion and I feel dejected. My inner power depletes, and my job feels tougher as I get weaker. Instead, if I think - I have challenges at office, but will face them - my positivity helps me to overcome them.

2. My Feelings Develop My Attitude. My thoughts create feelings at every moment whether in my relationships, workplace or in a shopping mall. Everyone is who they are,

everything is what it is. But how I feel about people and situations over a period develop my attitude towards them, determining whether I accept, respect or reject them. So, if I create a thought - I enjoy working in this office over a period - the resulting happiness defines my attitude about my office and creates a sense of belongingness.

3. My Attitude Brings Me into Action. My attitude dictates my outlook, behaviour, and response to people and situations. Thus my attitude drives my actions. Using the above example - I am an employee whose attitude towards my office is one of belongingness. This attitude brings me into action. I give my best performance. I work passionately and align myself with my company's goals.

4. Repeated Actions Form My Habits. Repeating any action twice, thrice, or ten times makes it a habit. When I am a high-performing employee, I enjoy all the associated benefits. It enhances my happiness and motivates me to do better in the next task, then the following task, and so on. I get into a habit of remaining happy, performing well and succeeding.

5. Habits Define My Personality. I become what I repeatedly do. All my habits combined shape my personality. They become an integral part of my life finding expression through my behaviour, and guide me through life. If I am a happy employee, it shows in my personality. In this way, my happiness is not restricted to my workplace, but accompanies me everywhere, leaving its impression in everything I do.

6. Personality in Action Manifests My Destiny. As will be my personality, so will be my every action. As will be my action, so will be the consequences of the action. That result is my destiny.

   This is how all elements come together - my thoughts create feelings, feelings develop my attitude, attitude comes into action, actions repeatedly done cultivate habit, habits influence my personality, and my personality scripts my destiny. Therefore, I choose how I want to feel the whole day, my whole life. I decide the list of emotions to use and the ones to avoid. I have the power to write a destiny of my choice. So, when I create a positive thought, it manifests a happy destiny.

   'If somebody offers you an amazing opportunity but you are not sure you can do it, say yes; then learn how to do it later!'

   - Richard Branson, Chairman Virgin Atlantic Airlines

Key Take Away

Anything big, assuming and conspicuous always, has its roots in something small, unassuming and inconspicuous. Living forms, made up of cells that are not even visible to the naked eye, are the best and easiest example to assert this truth. Even in its huge hulking state, a little change in the cell growth or formation can change the entire destiny of a life form. Despite its big presence, t is still the small underlying invisible cells that constitute and determine your living. The same holds true of success. Paving your destiny to success will grab everyone's attention and praise. The success story will always only talk about what you have come to be or do, and how your destiny has led you on to the top. What is easily missed out or not understood is that one's destiny is not paved by the big steps that one takes every once in a while. It is in fact shaped in every living moment with every little thought that one generates. The decision to think positive, constructive, imaginative, brave and life altering thoughts lies within you. You decide what to think, and what you think is what you become, which later shows how you face the challenges that life and work throws at you. And it is this attitude towards life that eventually paves your personality and your destiny – a destiny that determines if you will climb the ladder of success or be lost in the crowd.

'The only person you are destined to become is the person you decide to be.'

- Ralph Waldo Emerson

Chapter 6
Transforming Your Own Mindset

Growth Mindset and Fixed Mindset

A 'Growth Mindset' can change self and influence a change in others, too. A soul in such a mind learns from failure, and then converts the learning into success. This type of mind is thoughtful and continues to try something new. Such souls are not dampened by failures. They accept the challenges that they encounter.

In simple words, they simply 'Don't Give Up!' They are always ready to implement alternate approaches as they are fixated on success as their target. And once the target has been locked, all their guns fire and aim for the bull's eye to hit.

However, a majority of the crowd shows a propensity of having a 'Fixed Mindset'. Such souls are characterized with possession of narrow, limited and conservative approach that will never welcome change. Lack of confidence will further dampen their spirits and fetch only negative consequences. They will harbour a 'Chalata Hai... Chalega' attitude in their lifestyle.

Our aim should be to identify and seek people having 'Growth Mindset' if we are looking to build a team or adopt self-transformation practices that will fetch us success for ourselves. A person with a 'Growth Mindset', if nurtured properly will fetch unprecedented results. It has been well said that 'Respect for people is one of the secrets which can cause a revolutionary transformation in the way people live and work.' I am in complete agreement with the statement.

'Growth Mindset' people are self-motivated, and they possess high level of confidence. It is this understanding and attitude that can bolster the results of their endeavours.

Researcher Carl Dweck observes that a 'Growth Mindset' demonstrates the belief that intelligence can be trained and even basic abilities can be developed through dedicated hard work. On the contrary, a 'Fixed Mindset' portrays the belief that basic qualities like intelligence and talent are fixed traits.

'अगर राष्ट्र बदलना है, तो पहले अपना सोच बदलो !'

- Samrat Chandragupta Maurya (321–298 BCE)

Developing a Strong Personality

Each one of us wants to develop and own a personality that is perceived as charming and admirable. Organizations as a part of their training and development initiatives invest a lot to have their employees have a fair knowhow and necessity of grooming and personality development. Over the years of my career, I have aligned my agreement with the following mantra in making an impact.

Approximately 50% to 55 % of a first impression is based on appearance (dress, grooming, body language etc.) **(VISUAL); 40T to 35%** on the way we sound (the tone and pitch of our voice, accent, etc.) **(VOCAL);** and about 10 % on what we have to say **(VERBAL).** It is, thus, essential that we do everything possible on our part to ensure that we have not lost out on creating the **VISUAL** impact. Our professionalism, intelligence and the trust people form in us initially, is mainly due to our appearance. One may always argue that clothes and manners do not make the person but it is also true that the right match greatly improves the appearance.

Our tradition begins from the very first act of introduction - 'NAMASTE' - the world's most powerful and respectable way of greeting someone.

Making a good introduction leaves a favourable impression on others. In today's fast-paced business scenarios where international boundaries have almost disappeared, it is essential that we, as individuals, make sure that we are aware of norms and practices of cross-cultural sensitivity. One must recognize, interpret and correctly respond (and not react) to people, instances or situations that are prone to misunderstanding due to cultural differences.

As we move on to the next two parameters, i.e. vocal and verbal, I would reiterate that my readers start inculcating the aspect of assertiveness in their daily life. Assertiveness is the ability to express oneself and one's rights without violating the rights of others. A book on wellness quotes 'Assertiveness basically means the ability to express one's thoughts and feelings in a way that clearly states one's needs and keeps the lines of communication open with the other'. My readers who are entrusted with corporate roles will realize that this is one aspect that will help them induce a lot of maturity and create work-life balance in their endeavours. Practicing assertiveness will help a person know techniques in dealing with personal boundaries - their own and those of others while communicating with others. As a communication style and strategy, assertiveness is distinguished from both aggression and passivity as it is treated as a learned behaviour.

Passive communicators do not defend their own personal boundaries and, thus, allow aggressive people to abuse or manipulate them through fear. Passive communicators are also typically not likely to risk trying to influence anyone else. Aggressive people do not respect the personal boundaries of others and thus are liable to harm others while trying to influence them. A person communicates assertively by overcoming fear of speaking his or her mind or trying to influence others but doing so in a way that respects the personal boundaries of others.

There are two more aspects which I believe has a lot of relevance as far as developing of one's personality is concerned. They are listening and conversation. Listening according to me must make way for active listening, which is a way of listening that encourages the other person to talk. You may think that when you listen you do nothing. But that may not be true. Listening actively is important because it creates a mutual understanding between the speaker and the listener.

Conversation basics reinforce our listening skills. Let us make efforts to build our vocabulary and avoid vulgar references and swear words when we are in a conversation. In the process of getting to know and respecting one's personal space we should ensure that we do not get in too close. Utmost care should be taken to avoid personal questions and discussions on historical disasters. And when it comes to gossip, the rule is simple. Please keep it to yourself as everyone wants to hear about gossip until it's about them.

The competitive global business environment demands that etiquette, civility and grooming are given paramount importance in all interactions. Demonstrating good manners and etiquette is critical to winning a job, getting a promotion or scoring a deal. All it takes is an optimum balance of one's own skill, practice, good attitude and commitment to acquire and effectively utilize vital knowledge of how to act, carry oneself, and present one's talent. I urge my readers to make all efforts to package their image with strategic grooming for enhancing overall conduct during formal and informal interactions, thus portraying the right professional image to gain success. As is rightly said, ***'Good manners may open the doors that the best education may not.'***

Start Respecting to Earn Respect

If we try and to find out one secret which can transform the way people work and synergize within a team and across teams, maybe on personal front or professional front, one thing which directly comes to mind is respect for people, irrespective of their designations or any other parameter. The very fact that all human beings are the supreme creation of the visible force and magic called as nature, and well interpreted as God by people at large, speaks of the importance and value of each individual.

A person might be professionally at the lowest level doing a less significant job, but he is the head of the family back home, he is a brother, a father or maybe a son when it comes to his personal world. People acquire different designations based on their skill level, but the contribution of each team member is significant without which the team cannot strive to achieve its final goal. Imagine a scenario where there is no helping hand to assist us in a photocopying or documentation binding task (that is comparatively unskilled but yet it holds significance) especially when the submission is due for a major tender and we have so many pending tasks to complete to ensure that our submission is in order.

When people at large start respecting each other irrespective of their designations or so and when such a practice transforms into a culture, there would be less conflicts and misunderstandings. This would eventually add speed and smoothness to human life on personal as well as professional front. After all, human beings are the finest creation of the Almighty. We need to preserve their beauty. We need to ensure that we recognize and internalize the fact that like food, shelter, clothes, respect is also a psychological need of human beings globally. Let's start 'respecting people' and adopt it as a way of life, if we are not already doing so.

'Life should be great rather than long!'

- Dr. B.R. Ambedkar

Recognize Your Inner Power

I am an admirer of Peter Drucker, the management guru, and would like to share his following mantras of success!

a. Are you aware what you want to achieve?

   Because if you don't how what you want to achieve, then how would you be able to know whether your achievement has been fulfilled or not?

b. Plan for each step of your journey to achieve your goal.

c. To be successful is individual's responsibility

   Let's not forget the old saying 'where there is a will, there is a way'

d. Striving for success is always enjoyable

   I completely agree because whatever success I have personally achieved by now, though not an easy journey, but I always enjoyed striving for it. And once we taste success, enjoyment gets multiplied hundred times and it also motivates us.

e. Should ask for help whenever needed

If we are not able to achieve our goals, or we come across hurdles on the path to our goals, we should not hesitate to consult someone whosever has already reaped the fruits.

f. Avoid self-handicapping

Don't assume 'I can't'. Avoid negative feelings rather ask yourself 'why I can't?'

g. You need to be hungry

One must have desire for achieving success but to be the best, one need to feel the hunger, a burning sensation inside his stomach.

h. Doing it your own way

You need to develop your road map yourself and compete within. Though comparing with others (benchmarking) or say with the best must be done but putting your own mind may bring something different, something unique and maybe the best!

i. Instead of completing a journey or a task in one go it is better to focus only on the first step very carefully ensuring that quality is not compromised. Once the first step is successful others automatically follow. A good start to a task equals to the task half-done.

j. Execute your tasks together with all those who are involved, like a fun-filled activity.

k. Remain confident and motivated throughout your work journey.

l. Realize your strengths and start using those instead of bothering about the weaknesses.

m. Ensure that you are working on the right path and you are focused towards the goal because what ultimately will matter is the result.

n. Differentiate between Perfection and Effectiveness as your achievement of your target may be perfect but the same may not be effective in terms of adding value to your customers.

o. If you feel you are the only one who is struggling, then you are mistaken. There are many others in the race to achieve their goals. If you are finding it difficult to achieve your goal, then re-assess the path you have chosen and the strategies adopted. Modify them as may be appropriate and you will certainly win because you are born to win. Nobody can stop you. It's only a matter of time. Hence if needed, start afresh.

p. Ensure the right path and adopt the right strategies.

q. Learn from your mistakes. There is hardly any person who does not commit a mistake. Committing a mistake is natural and so instead of feeling bad or discouraged, learn from those and ensure there is no repetition of the same mistake. Every mistake is a lesson for the future.

r. Stretch out to achieve your goals. Instead of focusing only on the job look for other initiatives to ensure success. Keep revisiting your goals as well as the timelines allotted for achieving them.

s. Target your goals and adopt a path which is under your control. Avoid wasting your energy and time for matters that are beyond your control.

t. Have confidence in yourself, your beliefs, your faith and values and be self-motivated.

u. Try and be true to yourself.

v. Plan to reach out for something more than you can do or achieve. Have challenging targets and this you will keep you inspired all the time.

'He who does not have faith in himself can never have faith in God!'

- Guru Nanak

Purpose of Life versus Gap Analysis

What is the purpose of life? - a question that we often need to introspect. And if we are asking it from our heart, I have realized in my lifetime that the Almighty or an unknown power does help and guide us.

I do not regard myself as a great personality, but wherever I have worked, I have always craved to fetch an honest smile from my service seekers for my deliverables. I made it a point to observe their facial expressions. I could aptly judge whether their expressions in terms of their nod and smile were genuine or not as it is a universal truth that expressions never portray a false report. I wanted to ensure on every occasion that I was internally satisfied with my delivery of service; else, I considered it as a failure.

The parameters of quality for deliverables of a task are almost same across the industry. The lookout is for on-time completion at a minimal cost, something which all companies are struggling to achieve in present times. The problem lies in the fact that rather than adopting the right path and right approach, we get complacent and settle for short cuts. We start adopting an 'इत्न बहौत है' attitude. So, whom should we blame? We need to blame ourselves. Marginal benefits will always exist in all businesses. However, if we adhere to the right path with the right purpose, profitability is bound to grow which ensures a growth in the welfare of the people employed.

I recollect an occasion in a company wherein the implementation of 5S (Workplace Management) I witnessed generation of lot of scrap and unused machine parts which were eventually disposed of. I suggested that the funds generated from the scrap disposal be utilized for motivational purposes to reward the best workmen, the best 5S area, etc.

However, to my surprise, I was apprised that the amount was under the supervision and custody of 'Madam'. That was it. Now, who could dare to ask or make a proposal to 'Madam'? No one would dare or take any interest to suggest; who knows, she might have also agreed to the proposal.

The problem that lies here is why should we always blame 'Madam' or similar stakeholders? Was there anything that we could have done better? We were somehow limited in our moral visibility and opted for the easy path to earn as much as possible, without making the management acknowledge and realize the aspect of motivation and employee welfare. It is time that introspection starts to knock at the door, and we start listening to our conscience. 100% compliance to quality standards is the quest of everyone. And if we do invest our efforts and yet the outcome falls short of our expectation, then let's ask ourselves, 'Did we really want zero defect; and if so, did we ensure that everything that was necessary was fulfilled from our end?'

Let's now take time to introspect deeply because it's well said that the quality of everything is directly proportional to the quality of intentions. For instance, where our analysis concludes with wide gaps, it is a clear message that rework needs to be done on men, machine, material, methods and processes. The results need to be analysed further and we should continue with our efforts without giving up till we achieve our goals.

Key Take Away

The race of life is not very different from an actual race on a field. Remember those metre races or the relay races on our school sports day? Broaden your perspective, and you'll see life, in the big picture; life is still about running the race and reaching the end point. Ironically, though reaching the endpoint is what drives us in the race, we, honestly, never really want to reach the endpoint. The endpoint is burdened with an end that we don't want to reach, because after that there is no race to run. It is the race that goads us on and keeps us pushing towards the goal.

There are some who stumble and fall on the run, or some who lose pace, or stop to breathe.. But only the one who aims for success will be the one to carry on with the race, no matter how quick, fast, slow or how many times they stumble while racing. There will also be those who fall and attempt at rising. Hurt, panting and tired, they give up the race to think of their aches, niggles and sores. The situation is somewhat same in life and work too. For every hurdle, every obstacle, every failure, every miss, an actual winner would strive to find a way to get on top of it. Stopping is never an option for the ones heading towards success. Facing challenges head on and then untangling the difficult knot to march ahead with more confidence are the substance of success stories. The growth mindset is always the trump card of every successful man.

'Our greatest weakness lies in giving up. The most certain way to succeed is always to try just one more time.'

- Thomas Edison

Karma and Raja Yoga

(Compilation of teachings delivered by **BK Usha Didi** at Vile Parle, Mumbai in February'2020, BKs works of literature available on-line and the knowledge gained while listening Murlis)

The Philosophy

As stated in its most essential form is "As you sow, so shall you reap". "Every action causes an equal and opposite reaction". Each action is a seed planted, which comes to fruition according to time. Every second we perform an action.

Thoughts, words and deeds can be categorised across a wide spectrum, ranging from pure to impure. Their consequences occur in the immediate short term, mid-term and long term. They affect your body, mind, wealth, relationships, circumstances, opportunities etc. All actions are performed in the context of the consequences of previous actions which are often unknown to us, since performed in the past of another life time. Sometimes we do not see the connections and do not recognize that we are experiencing the consequences of a wrong action or set of actions we did or are continuing to do, in this life.

The knowledge of Raja Yoga as described by Brahma Kumaris (BKs) through the Murlis, includes a lot of information about Karma. 'Murli' is the recorded teachings spoken by the incorporeal supreme soul through his corporeal medium. Essentially, it states that a pure action brings about a beneficial result. An impure action brings about a result of loss. Whether we are soul conscious or body conscious makes all the difference to the quality of our actions.

Every soul exists within a perpetually turning cycle of cause and effect and acts according to their Sanskaras, which are produced by their Karma.

This is why God is called the Supreme Teacher, the Purifier, the Guide and the Knowledgeful One.

Life is not predestined as many of us believe. Instead one shapes his future by his own deeds (Karma).

As our thoughts are, so are our actions. Karma can be understood as a cycle of action and re-action.

Why someone attains outstanding worldly success? Why is one person extremely rich and many are poor, those who do not have food enough to even survive? Why did he do that to me? Does God decide life for everyone? Not at all!

The answers lie in one eternal truth based on the Law of Karma or Karma Philosophy - that no one can escape the result of his Karma. Depending on the bad or good Karma, or action or deeds one has to suffer or enjoy, either in this or the next life. There is no end to life. We are on an unlimited journey and will take the next birth according to the Karma we performed in the present life. The law of Karma is inviolable. Hence everyone must act with a sense of consciousness. We must acquire the right knowledge of what is good and what is bad.

The right Karma

The actions which are done with a pure intention, which first benefits the self and others and gives happiness to the world, and which pleases God is certainly the righteous deed.

The wrong Karma

If someone acts and gives sorrow to self or to others, or if even he pollutes the atmosphere with negative thoughts, he is doing an action which is opposite to the nature of soul.

The moral of the story is we need to do right Karma for our own benefit, not for showing to others.

Thoughts and Karma

Every action is preceded by thoughts. The most powerful instrument that mankind possesses is thought power. Thoughts build our consciousness and shape our attitude. One needs to know how important thoughts are. Every human creation we see in this world is due to powerful thoughts in human minds. Thoughts shape our world and are fertilized by knowledge.

The quality of thoughts determines the quality of our Karma. Karma in turn has a good or bad effect on us. This again influences our thinking. So right thinking based on right knowledge is essential for leading a peaceful and contented life. Raja Yoga meditation helps us in doing the right thinking … to be in the right path and right direction … helping to remain mentally strong amidst turbulent situations.

"What goes around … comes back around"

Raja Yoga

Rāja Yoga was both the goal of yoga and a method of attaining it. The term also became a modern name for the practice of yoga, when in the 19th century Swami Vivekananda equated Raja yoga with the Yoga Sutras of Patanjali.

It is a form of yoga chiefly concerned with controlling

and using the energy of the mind. It suggests the tool of meditation, slowing down the chaos of the mind so much that for an extended period of time, there is only one continuous thought. In due course of time, BKs understood the ultimate benefits of Raja Yoga for human beings and hence started propagating it across the world.

The Purpose-

Raja Yoga encompasses both body and mind, but the emphasis is more on mental and spiritual development.

Raja means King; a king acts with independence, self-confidence and assurance. Likewise, a Raja Yogi is autonomous, independent and fearless. It is a path of self-discipline and practice.

By regular practice, we may come out of various disorders in our character like Anger, Jealousy, Lust, Greediness, Selfishness, Criticism etc. which will certainly help us to achieve peace of mind and therefore lead to real happiness in life.

Eight Powers of Soul through Raja Yoga

Power to Accommodate

- is the ability to expand and accept the presence, ideas and desires of others.

Power to Tolerate

- is the ability to respond to external and internal events positively, yet not be affected by them.

Power to Face

- is the ability to confront and resolve external and internal obstacles, tests and challenges.

Power to Pack Up

- is the ability to bring things to an end and to stop wasteful thinking.

Power to Discriminate

- is the ability to discern the subtle and separate what is true from what is false.

Power to Judge

- is the ability to assess the quality of choices, decisions and actions in yourself and in others.

Power to Co-operate

- is the ability to give attention, time, experience and wisdom in the service of others

Power to Withdraw

- is the ability to step back and disengage from the world around you.

The Qualities/Virtues of the Soul

1. ***Purity*** - *the mother of Peace and Happiness*

2. ***Peace*** - *the natural stage of soul, thinking no burden, no question and no wasteful thought going in mind and thus have stillness.*

3. ***Love*** - *a natural feeling of a soul towards the supreme and all other souls. When self-realisation is achieved, we are connected with all living beings and consider the world as one family.*

4. ***Joy*** *- a momentous feeling of freedom and attainment, happiness is a natural feeling having peace and loving relationships in our life.*

5. ***Bliss*** *- the superior stage of happiness (joy), beyond any worldly feeling of happiness and sorrow.*

6. ***Powers*** *– spiritual, not physical.*

7. ***Knowledge*** *- the source of all virtues and the source is only one - the supreme soul.*

A materialistic world is not bad but we need to keep the essence of spirituality along with it. Resources are not bad but getting addicted to them is bad. Feelings and Consciousness, both are essential in life. Leading a life like a tortoise brings luck into one's life. If there is no peace, there can't be happiness.

Life is like a yagya and the process of involvement is Karma; let the fire of knowledge always burn inside. We put Jow and Til into it, Jow - the bad karmas and Til - the bad thoughts in mind, the Ghee - our wrong ways of getting money … let all these be Swaha! Whatever is done for the purification of life is the Karma Yoga.

We should try to keep ourselves aloof from wrong company of people and getting free from evils.

When you embrace pure knowledge, you will find the presence of joy, happiness, enthusiasm in life.

We need to always remember ~

- change yourself and your world will change.
- the one who co-operates receives co-operation
- to give happiness is a great art of charity

- simplicity is the hallmark of greatness
- speak less, speak sweetly, speak slowly, and speak wisely
- greater the humility, ... higher the achievement

Let us live well in this birth but also sow something good for the next birth.

LUCK is made of "every individual's Karma", and once made even God cannot revoke.

Your Notes/What do I need to clarify from the Author

May please approach the author at:
sapan_bardhan@rediffmail.com

Human Dignity

Human dignity is a sense of self-worth and the dignity in particular - a sense of pride in oneself. This conscious sense makes us feel that we deserve respect and honour from other human beings. It's one of the most important aspects of the human spirit, being valued and respected for what you are and what you believe in.

Dignity is the right of a person to be valued and respected for one's own sake and to be treated accordingly. Dignity also recognizes that all human beings possess a special value and have rights to create their own future. Dignity is the quality of being honourable, noble, excellent or worthy and regarded as the most supreme living creature. Dignity, in its appealing sense, is better referred to as human dignity. It is the conceptual basis for the formulation and execution of human rights. Each human should be regarded as a very invaluable member of the community.

We all try to teach our children the value of human dignity viz., respecting others, never to insult or put anyone down in public and conduct ourselves with decorum, etc. However they do not seem to understand, or if they do understand, they lack in demonstrating it through their own conducts.

Violations of human dignity in terms of humiliation refer to acts that humiliate or diminish human beings irrespective of their gender, religion, financial status, body colour and areas they belong too.

The topic of human dignity has hit the headlines world over several times in the recent past. Some of the practices that violate human dignity include torture, rape, social exclusion, labour exploitation, ragging in colleges, police atrocities in custody, bonded labour, slavery, etc. It also includes Poverty, Social Injustice, etc.

The legal perspective of the concept of human dignity was coined at the end of the Second World War. It has been regarded as the central perspective that discourses human rights. The Universal Declaration of Human Rights states that all humans have been born with equality in dignity and rights. For this reason, they are endowed with enough reason and pure conscience, hence should act towards one another with a deep spirit of brotherhood. In its preamble, the Universal Declaration of Human Rights seeks for recognition and respect for the inherent dignity as well as the equal and inalienable rights of every member of the human dignity, despite where they come from, their religious beliefs or background history.

The basic needs of a human being beyond the traditional ones of roti, kapda, aur makaan are pure drinking water, healthcare, cleanliness and sanitation and may be the availability of electricity considering today's requirements. The basic education of civic sense and skill development in the subjects of their own liking or choices through appropriate training and thereafter getting engaged in suitable income generating mechanism to take care of their own and family's livelihood, I personally feel they also constitute one type of human rights. This includes Equality, Security, Fair Justice, Fair opportunity for progress and Respect from the Society. Roti, Kapda and Makaan are the basic needs but the Process of giving and taking decides the dignity.

The behaviour of entrepreneurs and/or the senior management towards their workmen especially at lower level and how they take care of them, defines an organisation as a cultured organisation. Some industry leaders who have practiced human dignity at workplace like Sri Ratan Tata, Kumar Mangalam Birla, Azim Premji, Narayan Murthy, Anand Mahindra, Sushil Goenka, Inder T Jaisinghani & Brothers, Rajiv Bajaj are few out of many, I can remember!

India is blessed with a strong, sincere and visionary leadership. It will definitely achieve the desired level of human dignity in the time to come. This will also propel India to evolve as a world leader and superpower since taking adequate steps in promoting micro, small and medium scale industries to promote income-generating opportunities and hope will be able to resolve issues related to economic distribution to a large extent.

A CEO of a small scale industry mentioned during a seminar organised by Quality Council of India (QCI) at Pune that initially he used to directly look after the plant-related activities but gradually profitability started going down and started making loss. He analysed the reasons and changed the strategy, and even improved his own behavioural style and attitude towards the employees; he started taking care of their household requirements and children's education facilities and made employees completely free from worries so they could focus on the factory. Strategy worked as not only were the people very happy but profitability improved! This is a good example of valuing people's dignity.

India has one of the oldest and most civilised cultures in the world. Lot of positive learnings can be taken from our own ancient glorious past.

We have two great examples in our country of people who have dedicated their entire lives to ensure human dignity of others. Mother Teresa with her 'The Missionaries of Charity', whose primary task was to love and care for those people who nobody was prepared to look after. Another is Baba Amte for his commendable contribution towards the rehabilitation and empowerment of people suffering from leprosy.

At the end, please look at the photo shown below:

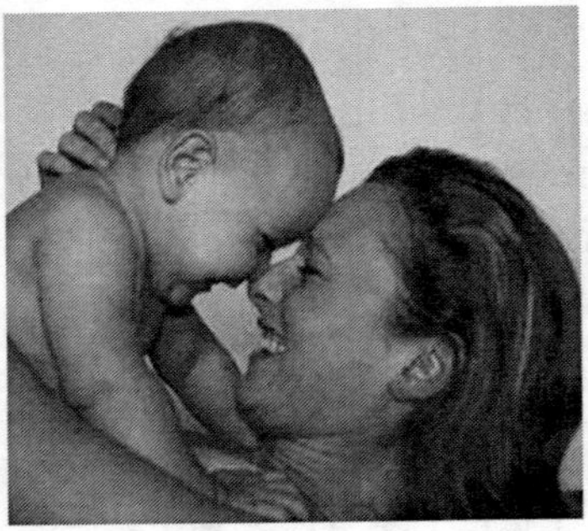

When a mother gives birth to a child, they all desire their children to live happily and future to be still brighter irrespective of the places they belong to around the world, their religion, financial status … poor or rich.,.

The lost children, orphans, etc., staying at Home Shelters or foster care also deserve good treatment from their respective in-charges and the society. In case we hear about bad treatment to them, we should all collectively protest and put efforts to gift them their right to dignity. Creating awareness among responsible people will certainly bring back their pride of doing Almighty's Work and receive blessings in turn.

Similarly, if we learn and practice being human, respecting others, wishing good to happen to others, think good for others forgetting our own egos … good will automatically come and you will have a happy and peaceful life.

***

Chapter 7
On Your Mark and Get Set for Your Journey

Once your vision and mission of life has been defined, start drawing a road map with a realistic timeframe and get prepared to start your journey in a new way using the guidelines as laid out in the subsequent chapters.

Dream and Aim High, But Plan in Detail

All individuals are born with a lot of potential, but unfortunately majority of them are not aware of their strengths. I believe that it is everyone's right to aim high and achieve their goals. This is possible once the right strategies are adopted and the necessary qualitative tools for the execution of the strategies are applied. It does not matter whether our goals are short term (a span of 1 to 4 years) or long term (a span of 5 to 15 years). The right strategy and appropriate tools will ensure achievement of our goals.

In order that we associate a sense of guarantee to our achievement of success, it is prudent that we have a plan in place at both the macro and the micro-level. We should also assess resources that will be necessary and adequate to execute our plans. The micro plan should have a time chart of activities that need to be accomplished on a monthly, weekly and daily basis along with the targets to be achieved. A simultaneous estimate of the resource demand in terms of men and machines are equally important. Let us be on our track and keep reminding ourselves the saying 'A Thinker, goes on thinking whereas a Doer starts moving while he is thinking'.

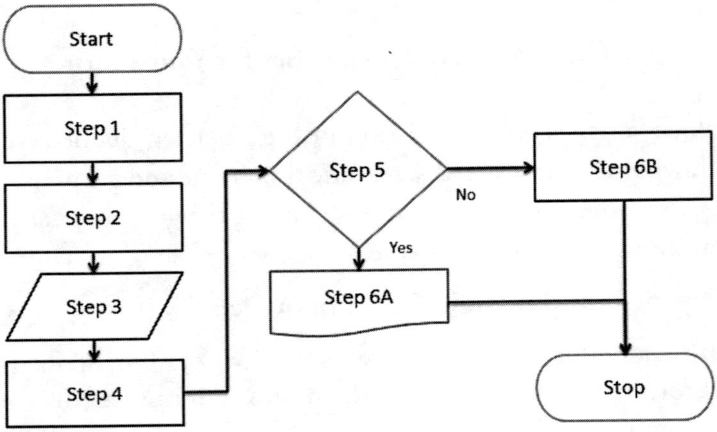

One can use the depicted indicative as a guide to chalk out their plan and customize the same to formulate their individualized plan. Steps 1 to 4 are plans one after another, whereas Step 5 in the diamond box is the verification part where the achievement of targets is validated, keeping quality in mind. Step 6 A means the output was satisfactory and completed at right time, whereas 6B refers to the corrected output which may need extra work hours to meet delivery timelines.

Ask Yourself - My Dream, My Vision and My Mission?

A management guru's words have now become a popular advice 'A Vision without an Action is a mere Dream'. In order to achieve success, one must have a dream that progresses towards a vision. However, the vision must be followed up by actions to ensure success in life.

And it is during this process of pursuing dreams that one will confront failures because of the mistakes that were committed. This is the juncture where we should not get bothered and worried, because mistakes build our experience, and experience thereby reduces our mistakes. If one can learn from his/her mistakes, then others learn from their success.

My story has been nothing different. I faced a lot of hurdles in my professional career too, but I never gave up. And now that I have been successful, I wonder how I have achieved success. Every individual must have a mission statement for their life. It is the purpose of their life. Mother Teresa had a mission to serve mankind. If we wish to be successful in life, we must be successful at both the professional and personal front, which includes his/her family also. The thought of doing something good for the society and nation will be a gift of completeness for every individual. As Indians, we have since ages as a part of our culture, fostered the value of 'Rashtra Dharma' followed by 'Karma Yoga' with utmost importance. Lord Krishna quotes in the Gita - 'कर्मण्येवाधिकारस्ते मा फलेषु कदाचन' and I am firm believer and follower of the preaching.

Vision without action is a mere dream; action without vision is just a time pass.

'Vision with action is success and can change the world'

- Joel A Barker

Know Your Customers and Stakeholders

A customer in simple terms is defined as the 'recipient or beneficiary of goods or services'. It is an irony that the above fact though is easily understood, but seldom is accepted and practiced. People by and large use the word 'customer' to relate to organizations with whom they have a business transaction. Every transaction in a broad sense involves a buyer and a seller. However, a minute's observation will make us realize that the role of 'customer' gets swapped between both the actors, i.e. the buyer and the seller during the individual tasks that they perform as part of the transaction. For example, a seller delivers goods and services to a buyer (i.e. his 'customer') and the buyer in turn must pay back for his purchase. In a sense, the seller now becomes a recipient of a service or goods (i.e. the payment transfer or the cash money) from the buyer. So, it is evident that the role of 'customer' swapped among the buyer and seller when viewed from the above perspective. Along similar lines, an organization is a 'customer' for its employees, as the employees deliver their services to the organization. However, the employees also become the 'customer' of the organization as they become the beneficiary of availing a safe, caring and a rewarding work environment.

A 'stakeholder' is a person with an interest or concern in the business. Stakeholders can be creditors, directors, employees, suppliers, governmental agencies, owners, communities etc. They can affect or be affected by the organization's objectives, policies and actions.

Of the three processes of TQM, i.e. Quality Process, Management Process and People process, the foremost and the most important process is the Quality Process as the journey towards excellence begins from there. It calls for understanding the 'Needs and Expectations of the Customer' and aligning one's effort to make sure that the needs and expectations are met completely and correctly. An aspect worth considering is that it is not only about identifying and listening to the needs and wants, but also 'understanding' them. Once the needs and wants are understood, all that is needed is to put the understanding into the management process of 'PDCA (Plan Do Check Act) Cycle' as defined by Dr. Edward W Deming. The problem starts creeping in when we do not understand the needs and wants with complete clarity and yet start executing our actions.

A mail delivery person once left a 'Sorry, we missed you' sticker on my door. I was out of my house for only a few minutes and maybe the mail delivery person visited me during that duration. I thought that the person would be in close vicinity making his other deliveries as much time had not elapsed. I decided to call him, but surprisingly the sticker did not have any contact number. In short, the delivery person did perform his/her duty of putting the sticker at my door but failed to understand as to what might be my need and want after reading the message on the sticker. The concept of 'customer' is thus relevant to all spheres of our life. Whether it is the community where we dwell in, or the roads on which we drive, or the goods and services that we avail from civic bodies; the customer-centric requirements, or better termed as the needs and wants of a 'customer', always exist.

Understanding Customers' Requirements

The requirements of the customers hover around the aspects of best quality and on-time delivery at minimal costs. Customers pay us for the products and services that they source from us as suppliers. They can't be dictated. Their needs and wants are the very reason for our existence. They have stringent requirements in terms of quality, cost and delivery. One must also gauge and understand the various hidden expectations that are usually associated with a customer but are usually not expressed.

One of the processes for attaining quality as detailed in the TQM approach is to know customer requirement. Getting to know about the requirement of the customer is important but what holds more significance is understanding the requirement very clearly, including the potential requirement. A prime reason that funnels down to customer dissatisfaction thereby impacting the business financials is the delay associated with production and manufacturing due to an improper understanding of the requirements.. A casual approach towards understanding and interpreting the details of customer requirements will result in increased cost, and poor quality and will also contribute to tarnishing of the brand and business image. It is also necessary that wise and experienced personnel be associated with tasks which are simple, yet are so significant in nature that if executed erroneously will cause substantial damage.

Let us consider a few examples. Assume that two trucks of load were scheduled to leave for their destinations, one for Chennai and another destined for Chandigarh. The task of dispatch scheduling was not given due importance and was left to a worker with low skillset and lack of job know-how. The worker just did the opposite of what had to be done. So, the trucks were now set to leave for their destinations that were completely opposite to where they should have headed for. Somehow, the involvement of an individual who went overboard beyond his area of responsibility noticed this flaw and corrective action was taken before the trucks departed. Imagine the impact of cost, time delay and customer dissatisfaction that would have cropped up had the mishap not been averted. What went wrong was a very simple act of understanding the requirement and having the right know-how for task execution.

A contract has just been finalized between a customer and his supplier. After a few days, the customer got in touch with the supplier's representative and made a specific request to have an additional imprint of his logo on the deliverable item. The supplier personnel accepted the request but owing to his busy schedule, missed to intimate this additional requirement to the manufacturing team. The customer's quality inspector could not find the logo during his visit and had no other option but to reject the clearance of the finished product. Another classic case wherein the requirement though understood was not documented and included in the job list and subsequently got left out from the quality assurance procedure of the manufacturing plant.

In his attempt to record the voice of customer, a customer care executive from a restaurant brand called up a customer and enquired about his recent experience of dining at one of its outlets. The customer care executive had picked up the correct date and time of the visit of the customer but unfortunately did not take care to note the exact cuisine that the customer had opted during his visit. So apparently it was a customer feedback being sought for a product that was not availed. The experience for the customer went downside when he had to keep insisting that did not have the food for which his opinion was being sought for. Imagine the embarrassment for the customer if there were religious faiths of prohibition associated with the food that was discussed. Such mistakes may have made the customer from calling off his future visits to the restaurant. In this case there was no mistake with the product and service on the day of delivery but a half-hearted feedback call which as a practice of customer care went wrong fetching unwanted results.

The solution to overcome such instances is to ensure that we are prepared with all facts and figures before we initiate our conversation with our customers. Quite often, the best way to assist in our preparedness of dealing with our customers is to think like one. .

In short, put yourself in the Customer's Shoes, only then you will know where it pinches and hurts.

Aiming for Customer Delight ? Think Differently!

Thinking differently means planning and adopting ways and methods very different than the routine ones to achieve results that score better on qualitative and quantitative parameters. These methods are efficient as compared to their routine counterparts and are usually an outcome of experimentation and out of the box thinking. In an organization the senior management should constantly think and chalk out something new and innovative and in their process encourage people.

To ensure that thinking differently yields a better result, we need to get started with working differently so that we think differently. Maasaki Imai, the quality guru who pioneered the Kaizen process stresses on 'Change for the better'. According to Maasaki Imai - Kaizen is a participative and democratic approach that involves every employee – from upper management to lower staff - for every activity, considering the future vision and building the organization into a dynamic one. Such an organization will always remain on top of the world.

Let me share an incident that happened in Japan. A customer registered a complaint with the customer care division about an empty soap box. The company took the complaint seriously and dedicated the matter to the team of engineers to work out a solution. The engineers ended up installing high resolution x-ray machines at every stage to avoid the flaw of an empty box escaping through. The same problem later occurred in another company. The staff of that company simply used a high-speed fan to serve as a blower at the exit point to identify if at all any empty box had come across till the final stage.

By now you must have guessed it. Yes, the second company designed a solution for the problem that was cost effective and secure. Owing to our experience and expertise, many a times we start looking at every problem in a very complicated manner but sometimes simplicity takes us closer to the solution effectively.

Jack Welch in his book, Winning, has spoken of simplicity as one of the principles towards successful decision making. Thus, when we think differently many problems can bottle down to simpler ones thus resulting into simple and right solution. Shri N R Narayana Murthy, Smt. Sudha Murthy and Shri Ratan Tata are a few among many personalities who display simplicity and radiate the comfort of others to approach them. The best approach to simplicity is to try and think differently when one has given up thinking critically.

Let me cite another example which recently came under my notice. All of us watch a lot of talent shows aired in various television channels. The show is hosted by an anchor who runs down every episode from start till the end. While I admire the effort of every anchor of such shows, I would like to highlight

Shri Manish Paul who hosted the show, 'Indian Idol' aired by Sony TV. To me, he has given a new dimension to the entertainment that the show brings up. His efforts towards small talks, humour and fun activities have contributed to make the show interesting and, in turn, achieving viewer delight in true sense. If one makes a candid observation, it will truly be justified to conclude that his contribution has an equal significance as compared to those of the participants, the judges, the celebrities and not to miss the musicians towards the successful show packaging of each episode. While the Target Rating Point (TRP) fetches favourable indices, this is another example of fetching customers delight.

Let us always follow the approach of (n + 1) where 'n' stands for giving something extra or stretching that extra mile to achieve delight. The quality and quantity of 'n' depends on individual effectiveness, efficiency and specifically what and up-to what extent one would like to offer.

Recently, I moved to another saloon and I was happy to observe the cleanliness around, facility of having a washroom, enough time being devoted instead of hurrying for the next customer to sit, music in a low volume and customer care attitude. After a few months, when I was in the market, the old saloon owner came running to me and enquired why I was not going to his shop. I replied I found a better saloon, that too at a lower price. He continued telling me that I was a customer of long standing of over 9 years. Surprisingly, it was not his mood that made me switch over to a new one ... but to teach him a lesson so that he improves, and customers come back to him.

So, customers' requirements are changing. Had that new shop

not come there I would have continued with the old one. Customers always look for better options.

Give customer more than what he expects. ***He will be yours for life.***

Assess Your Strength and Start Using Them

Human beings have a very peculiar nature when it comes to identifying their own strengths and good qualities. In majority of instances, they are unaware of the qualities they possess. So, the question of using them simply does not arise. The same phenomenon may be applicable to you too.

I would suggest that on a fine morning as per your convenience you should sit at a relatively quiet place and begin to pray to God and seek his help to guide you. It is evident that you will undergo introspection. I suggest that you write down the same on a piece of paper. You should come out with a list of good qualities and habits that you possess but have not been able to make use of due to some or the other reason. Once you are done with such a list, start using those strengths and good qualities in your everyday life.

Observe yourself and I am sure you will find a change. A positive change in yourself and your confidence will start building, bringing a smile on your face that you were longing for.

Identify Your Weaknesses and Convert Them to Strengths

Just as you carried out the exercise to know your strength and good qualities, be true to yourself and conduct a similar exercise to know your weaknesses. Seek help of the Almighty to identify your grey areas where you would like to improve.

Have a flash back of your memories and start writing what you feel are your weaknesses.

You will be comfortable and eager to proceed on a self-improvement journey as you yourself do not like the items that you have shortlisted on the list. Believe it folks; once you are done with this part, you have completed the most difficult part of the exercise. Now select a convenient day, place and time, preferably the early morning hours. Sit to meditate and with a deep breath pray to God. Ask him to help you get rid of your weaknesses one by one. You never wanted them in your life, and you have realized that they are creating hurdles on your path to success. Repeat this practice every day without fail believing in Your sub-conscious mind will be your guide and very soon you will observe that your list has changed and is left with a favourable balance where your strengths and good qualities have substantially outnumbered your weaknesses. The world will start changing for you, and in fact you have boarded the journey to change yourself.

Chapter 8

The Culture Building

Teamwork is mandatory for us to achieve success. A team that resonates the feeling of mutual support and empathy truly demonstrates the saying 'together we win'. Team building and thereby nurturing a culture of teamwork is a huge area of improvement for many organizations. Often we come across instances wherein we lose focus of our vision and mission and start an unwanted tussle among us to prove out our individual supremacy. This leads to a sense of uncertainty within us and when we are not certain how we can dream to achieve our target?

During my career, I have come across many seniors who have not taken time to mentor and develop their juniors into a unified team. . Such individuals never feel the need to delegate authority and want them to be referred or consulted for every decision, no matter how small it might be. This whole act and way of working is a parasite within the organization which slowly retards the growth process. It is due to this very reason that when we grow as seniors, we need to inculcate the habit of teamwork and developing ourselves as a good team player.

Knowledge and Skill Development

The enhancement of skills remains the main focal point of our journey to success. The ideal skills are categorized as - Technical, Functional, Managerial, Knowhow of Integrated Management Systems, Problem Solving Tools/Techniques and Behavioural. Skill development is one of the most important aspects of our lives. College education does help to get a job or assists in starting up a business; but for ensuring success, an individual must upgrade his/her knowledge on a continual basis. He or she should be on the constant look out for acquiring additional knowledge and skills to get better results at work site.

We all are aware that we need skilled workforce at work site. Skill comes from knowledge. Once the right skills and knowledge is implemented, the results are clearly visible. The urge to better our results drives the necessity for upgrading our set of skills. It would be good and optimum for all of us to follow the cycle of 'Learning – Un-learning – Re-learning'. I recollect an individual referring to basic education like a pizza base which does not bring out the real taste. The delicacy and flavours are relished from the various toppings spread on the pizza base. In similar lines, we too need to keep adding the toppings of skill and knowledge enhancement over our own pizza base to succeed in today's competitive market.

Skill and knowledge enhancement will have its own cost. I suggest everyone to allocate a defined budget for enhancement of one's knowledge and skill which will certainly pay back in the days ahead. A common myth carried by everyone is that, it is the management's responsibility to impart training. This myth must change. The choice must be ours to get trained. Over the years, I have invested substantially on knowledge enrichment and fetched a higher return in my work life.

Continual learning is an activity of self-motivation. In an organization, it is necessary that the senior management takes time to plan and provide training to the workforce as per job requirements. The whole process will be highly effective if adequate time is spent on identifying actual training needs by analysing the qualitative and quantitative output of each process and thereby contribute to the process of meaningful value addition.

Let us keep reminding that higher the competency of staff, higher would be the number of quality deliveries thereby resulting in higher profitability. But in my experience, I have observed that many of the immediate bosses do not want to send their executives and workmen, despite nominated by themselves and organized by training department. The reason being the work may suffer, need to submit a report, or give a presentation to top management. A few intelligent ones nominate some other person just to maintain the number game though the training subject may not be so relevant to those. Thus, this very important aspect of people development and thereby organization development, only remains on paper .... HR showing 100% compliance since they also find themselves helpless.

Many senior executives have a feeling that they don't need any training as they have so many years of experience. I remember even today that after receiving training, on TQM concepts, when we joined back office, we were asked to give presentation to the senior management as a part of their training inputs and it was made mandatory for all of them to attend the one day program. Time was from 9.30 am to 5.00 pm.

First day, very few people attended. A message was sent to the Executive Director's Office. He asked our boss to send the list of participants who had turned up by 10 am. Boss followed the instruction; result was within next half an hour attendance was full and the system was followed for all the programs. This is 'Top Management', ensuring whatever needed is planned and achieved on time.

Please remember learning is an investment.

I am reproducing below here a module, developed by me and published by ASQ, Ahmedabad in November 2016

People Transformation for 'Kaushalya Nipun' through Education & Training

- a Risk Based Thinking

('Mission Eklavya' - Determination to Learn)

One of the essential aspects for continual growth of every human being and thereby growth of all organizations and society at large is the Education & Training.

For continual improvement, organizations opt for ISO Management Systems, Total Quality Management, Total Productive Maintenance, Lean etc. The good thing is that all systems, techniques, philosophies give utmost importance to Skill Enhancement. All management gurus also emphasize on up-gradation of skills on continual basis irrespective of nature of business or levels in an organization. This is essentially needed to meet newer requirements/expectations of customers that are changing with times. 'Customer delight' is the only mantra for any organization to face the competitive challenges of current and future global needs.

However, over a period it has been experienced that this important requirement that is critical for business success remains on paper in majority of cases and this seldom happens because of consideration of 'On-Job process requirements' while identifying training needs.

Once a person joins an organization, his/her set of skills must be mapped with the organizational requirements, vision and mission and also considering the past and potential failures, gaps identified and thereby the training needs are planned looking at the criticality or risks an organization might have in case of non-fulfilment of customer requirements and non-alignment with organization's vision.

Therefore a procedure and a module has been developed to calculate the value of Risk Priority Number (RPN) using the good concept of Failure Modes and Effects Analysis. The various processes are divided into Sub-processes which are then assessed with associated risks against Occurrence, Severity and Detection (effectiveness of current control) in the scale of 1 to 4.

Thus, looking at the higher RPNs, prioritization of processes/ sub-processes which are critical to organization's success is done. Once prioritized process/sub-processes are worked out, those are examined to identify the likely activities responsible for higher risks and skills needed to improve the output of the processes. The requirement of organizing training is then mapped (competency/skill mapping) with all concerned employees in four categories i.e. 1. Technical/Functional 2. Management (ISO/GMP & IT) Systems 3. Behavioural (attitudinal). 4. Contribution in achieving organization's goals/mission/ vision or any other priorities.

An easy to operate module formatted with various colour codes having an option for 'Evaluation of Training Effectiveness' has been developed for organizations, desirous to enhance all round skills of their people.

The above process/module is quite different than our traditional training method and is likely to ensure organization meeting their goals in terms of P (productivity), Q (quality), C (cost), D (delivery), S (safety), M (morale) etc. The model if adopted and implemented honestly, provides all concerned an opportunity to up-grade their skills on a continual basis, adding value to the society and making India much stronger. Module to ensure all Corporate and the Country's objective of 'Zero Defect & Zero Effect' with improved profitability through 'Loss & Wastes Elimination' through People Development.

6i - B

		Calculation of RPN (Risk Priority No) by the Process/Sectional I/c & Unit Heads *(Ref: Chapter 6 - B)*													Document ID :			
															Rev. No. : 00		Issue Date :	
Sr. No.	**Process**	**Activities**	**Technical/Functional**				**Management/IT System**				**Behavioural**				**Vision/Mission/Mfg. Excellence/TPM**			
			Occurance/ Likelyhood (a1)	**Severity (b1)**	**Current Control(c1)**	**RPN (A) (a1 x b1 x c1)**	**Occurance/ Likelyhood (a2)**	**Severity (b2)**	**Current Control (c2)**	**RPN (B) (a2 x b2 x c2)**	**Occurance/ Likelyhood (a3)**	**Severity (b3)**	**Current Control (c3)**	**RPN (C) (a3 x b3 x c3)**	**Occurance (a4)**	**Severity (b4)**	**Current Control (c4)**	**RPN (D) (a4 x b4 x c4)**
1	RM Reciept	Gate Entry	2	4	3	24	2	3	2	12	2	3	2	12	2	2	2	8
		Qty Verification	4	2	2	16	4	2	2	16	4	2	2	16	4	2	2	16
		Quality Check	2	2	1	4	2	2	1	4	2	2	1	4	2	2	1	4
		COA Checking	3	3	3	27	3	3	3	27	3	3	3	27	3	3	3	27
2		A																
		B																
		C																
		D																
3		A																
		B																
		C																
		D																
4		A																
		B																
		C																
		D																
5		A																
		B																
		C																
		D																

6i - A

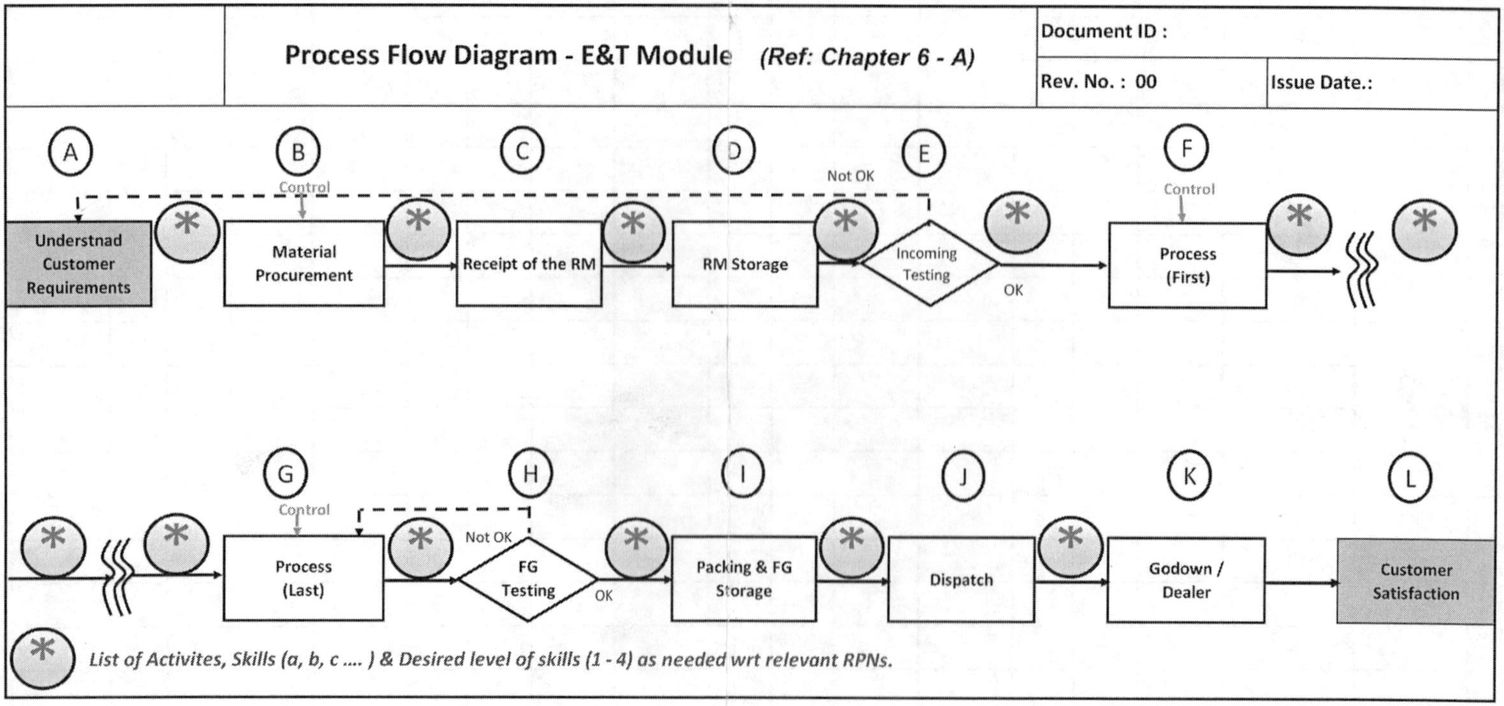
Process Flow Diagram - E&T Module (Ref: Chapter 6 - A)
Document ID :
Rev. No. : 00
Issue Date.:
A
B
C
D
E
F
Control
Not OK
Control
Understnad Customer Requirements
Material Procurement
Receipt of the RM
RM Storage
Incoming Testing
OK
Process (First)
G
H
I
J
K
L
Control
Not OK
Process (Last)
FG Testing
OK
Packing & FG Storage
Dispatch
Godown / Dealer
Customer Satisfaction
List of Activites, Skills (a, b, c ....) & Desired level of skills (1 - 4) as needed wrt relevant RPNs.

6i - C

		Process: (Ref: Chapter 6 - C) Calculation of RPN (Risk Priority No) by the Process / Sectional I/c /Unit Heads	Document: ID			
			Rev. No.: 00		Issue Date	
Sr. No.		Activities/Skills	Occurance Likelyhood (a)	Seveity (b)	Current Control (c)	RPN (a x b x c)
1	RM Reciept	Gate Entry / a, b, c, d ...				
		Qty Verification / a, b, c, d ...				
		Quilty Check / a, b, c, d ...				
		COA Checking / a, b, c, d ...				
2		A				
		B				
		C				
		D				
3		A				
		B				
		C				
		D				
4		A				
		B				
		C				
		D				
5		A				
		B				
		C				
		D				

6i - D

RPN: Occurrence X Severity X Current Control
Impacting on Safety, Quality, Delivery, Cost, Morale etc.

Level		**Likely % (CFT to decide)** *... may vary from plant to plant*	
Occurrence & Severity			
4. High	☹	11 –	≥15%
3. Moderate	☹	06 –	10 %
2. Little	😐	01 –	05 %
1. Nil	☺	0%	
Current Control			
4. Very Weak	☹		
3. Weak	☹		
2. Good	😐		
1. V. Good	☺		

Category (Ref: ....)	**Examples ...**
Technical / Functional	Product & Delivery Failure/ increased cost etc.
Management / IT System	Inconsistency of product, delay in delivery, Increased COPQ etc.
Behavioural	Accidents, creating negative environment etc.

Vision /Mission/Mfg. Excellence/ TPM
(Trends)

- Goals/Objectives
- Profit margin
- Customer satisfaction
- M/C Up-time
- Good Will in the market
- Etc.

6i - E

Competency/Skill Matrix - Mapping *(Ref: Chapter 6 - E)*

Document ID :	
Rev. No. :	Issue Date :

Unit:	Grade :	Process :

Employee Code	Tech. / Functional (*Ref: RPN'A')								Mgmt. / IT System (* Ref: RPN 'B')				Behavioural (*Ref: RPN 'C')				Vision/Mission/ Mfg. Excellence/ TPM (*Ref: RPN 'D')			
	T-1 / F-1	T-2 / F-2	T-3 / F-3	T-4 / F-4	T-5 / F-5	T-6 / F-6	T-7 / F-7	Average (2015-16)	MS-1	MS-2	MS-3	Average (2015-16)	B-1	B-2	B-3	Average (2015-16)	V-1 / M-1	V-1 / M-2	V-1 / M-3	Average (2015-16)
* Desired Level of Skill (1-4) as per RPN	3	3	3	4	3	3	3	3	4	2	4	3	4	2	4	3	2	3	4	3
10001	1	1	1	3	4	4	4	3	2	4	2	3	2	4	2	3	2	4	2	3
10002	2	2	2	2	2	3	2	2	2	2	2	2	2	2	2	2	2	2	2	2
10003	2	2	3	2	3	1	2	2	2	2	3	2	2	2	3	2	2	2	3	2
10004	1	1	2	1	2	2	1	1	1	1	2	1	1	1	2	1	1	1	2	1
10005	1	1	1	1	1	2	1	1	1	1	1	1	1	1	1	1	1	1	1	1
10006	2	4	2	4	2	1	1	2	2	4	2	3	2	4	2	3	2	4	2	3
10007	2	2	2	2	2	3	2	2	2	2	2	2	2	2	2	2	2	2	2	2
10008	2	2	3	2	3	1	2	2	2	2	3	2	2	2	3	2	2	2	3	2
10009	1	1	2	1	2	2	1	1	1	1	2	1	1	1	2	1	1	1	2	1
10010	1	1	1	1	1	2	1	1	1	1	1	1	1	1	1	1	1	1	1	1

Employee Code	Trainiing Needs / Evaluation of Effectiveness (within 3-6 months of training)							
	1		2		3		4	
	Training Code	Evaluation of Effectiveness	Training Code	Evaluation of Effectiveness	Training Code	Evaluation of Effectiveness	Training Code	Evaluation of Effectiveness
* Desired Level of Skill (1-4) as per RPN								
10001	T2	2	T3	4	T5	4		4
10002	T7	2		5		3		4
10003		2		3		3		3
10004		1		3		3		3
10005		4		4		4		4
10006		5		5		5		5
10007		3		3		3		3
10008		4		4		4		4
10009		3		3		3		3
10010		3		3		3		3

6i - F

E & T (Education & Training): Rating Criteria

*** considering individual's current level of competence/ skill and its positive/adverse impact on the organisation (objectively captured by the respective Process/Sectional I/C)**

4 (Very Good):

Mastered the subject pertaining to his/her area of operations / functions, performs / delivers very well independently as per requirements and intended results. Uses analytical and problem solving skills when needed, has ability to teach and lead other teams and also has a fair knowledge of overall process.

3 (Good):

Understands the subject pertaining to his / her area of operations / functions and performs / delivers well independently, as per requirements and intended results. Uses analytical and problem solving skills as and when needed.

2 (Fair):

Understands the subject pertaining to his / her area of operations/functions and performs / delivers satisfactorily, as per requirements & intended results but needs guidance / supervision by superiors.

1 (Unsatisfactory):

Neither able to perform / deliver as per requirements and intended results even under guidance / supervision of superiors nor understands the subject well.

***

6i - G

(Ref: Chapter 6 – F)

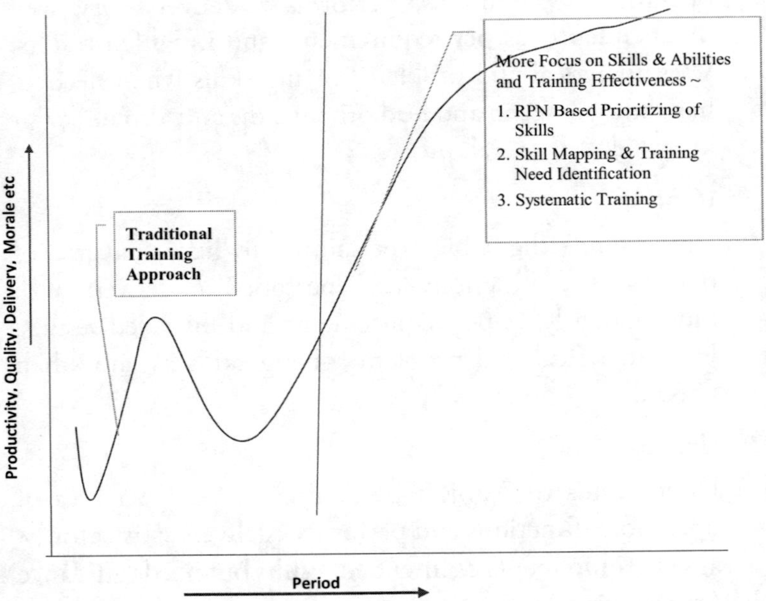

Like icebergs, most of the problem is usually below the surface! Looking at it positively – we may even get diamonds - so what do we need to do?

We need to dive deep into the sea to identify or anticipate the likely issues, which eventually may cause risks, solve the existing issues and plan encountering the issues which are likely to become threats to our business later. Quite ahead of any risk to get surfaced out and we get better results in the form of diamonds!

Lesser issues, lesser internal failures, higher customer satisfaction and enhanced number of loyal customers increased margin of profit!

Diving deep enhances level of skills nearer to perfection boosting up Self Confidence and thereby Self Esteem needed to live with pride and dignity!

To be Disciplined

The word 'discipline' we must have started listening from our parents especially fathers, since they used to take care of external world, basically the earning source of the family. Now of course the situation has changed, and majority of women have started earning too, a good change in the country.

Coming to the word discipline, it normally means people obeying rules or standards of behaviour or even following code of conducts; and in order to be successful this is one of the pre-requisites ?

Examples:

Attending work places on time, having food more or less on time either at workplaces or at home, obeying the instructions of superiors, driving vehicles according to the speed defined for particular roads/highways, obeying traffic rules, sleeping and getting up in the morning, morning or evening walks as per usual practice, completion of tasks as planned etc.

Military Department or even Police Forces are great examples of discipline. Once a course of action is decided, everybody involved needs to follow; march means march, shoot means shoot, and if not obeyed this would be considered as indiscipline.

Discipline is also a good base of any cultured family, institutions, factories, offices etc. Discipline supports people to be successful, wherever they are. In fact, a disciplined approach also helps reduce tension resulting in healthy blood pressure and sugar levels.. It develops a sense of confidence which is very much visible on the face.

The current industrial business scenario is throwing a lot of challenges on us, demanding managers to step up as leaders, sooner the better. This has led to the need for competencies such as managing generation gaps, dealing with difficult employees positively, multiskilling, conflict resolution etc. It's like progressing from a manager to a leader, specialist to generalist, analyst to an integrator, tactician to a strategist, bricklayer to an architect, problem solver to agenda setter, warrior to diplomat and supporting team members to play a lead role.

There's more danger in not training and developing people.

There is a famous quote where CFO asks:

What happens if we train them and they leave?

The perplexed CEO says: What happens if we don't and they stay? It's about developing a Profitable Culture

Competency Iceberg

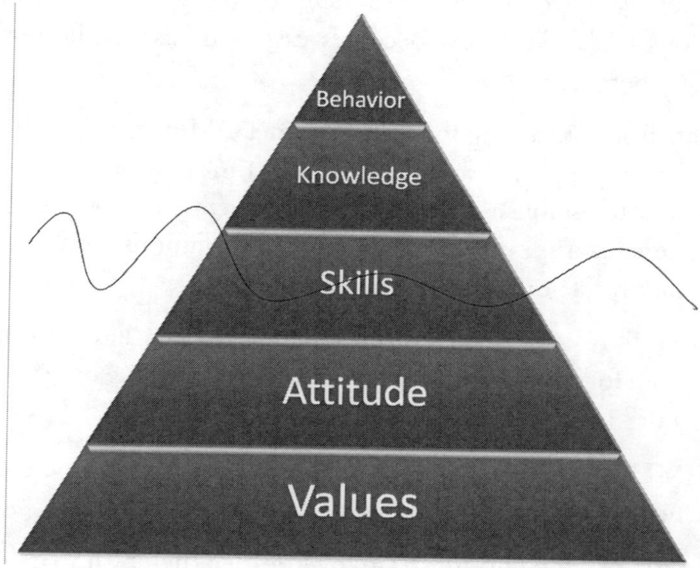

The focus here is to build a profitable culture rather than building to be on the path of Look at the picture of an iceberg known as Competency Iceberg!

As we have repeatedly discussed the 'people first' approach and taking care of their welfare, but to be profitable we need to have people whore are not only of academically qualified but also have the basic values in place and of course a very high level of positive attitude, to take the team along with, develop them for enhanced set of skills, think for the organization rather than individual high packages.

During interviewing a person, we can only observe his or her immediate behaviour, level of knowledge only to have a profitable culture within an organization; we need people having those qualities, other than skills for action on site.

Once, we have the above system in place implementing various tools like below becomes easy and sustainable for a longer period.

Apart from practicing the well-known TQM principle of 'Do right things right, first time and every time', an organization in order to establish an integrated management system across the organization needs to practice the famous and most popular result-oriented Japanese tool '3 M'.

- ✓ MUDA which means minimizing wastes like waiting time for transports, in-process, inventories, raw materials, work in progress, finished goods etc.
- ✓ MURA which means inconsistencies in processes, products etc.
- ✓ MURI which means strain /overburden thereby impacting ergonomics

The above internationally harmonized best practices are needed to optimize operational cost and increase profitability which is one of the core objectives of any business.

The above statements are true for getting monetary benefits or increasing margin of profit, but what we are talking here is about a culture - a profitable culture!

Swami Vivekananda did not talk about economics, but it's said that he used to suggest about building Human Capital through education, building skills and capabilities towards material prosperity. According to him material prosperity is required before moving towards spirituality.

What we need to have a strong belief on

A system based on values, a system of people-focused management, a system of respecting all human beings irrespective of their levels, caste and creed, a system focused on customer delight, a system of total quality management thus creating an environment; to have an aura of mutual trust and thinking of ethically earning profit for the organization because objective of TQM is earning more profit so as to open more number of organizations and providing employment opportunities to the people at large - caring for the society, uplifting them and contribute to nation-building!

Once we start believing and working as stated above, culture building takes momentum and ensures dividends in future.

Planning For Work-Life Balance

In today's fast-moving environment, most of us are running a rat race to live a very comfortable life, maybe more comfortable than what may be required. The requirements go on increasing every day, every moment and we are on the lookout for jobs that fetch us higher financial packages. A higher paying job demands greater time devotion and it often leads to the syndrome of thinking only about work thereby compromising the time we should have instead spent with our family members or would have done something contributory to the society.

Earning money is a must but are we not becoming too much self-centred? It often seems that our only objective is to go up and up in the corporate ladder and get better financial packages. The mind gets engulfed in a monotonous thought process to keep on stretching an extra mile in order to pacify the management of one's contribution towards compensating the cost at which he/she has been hired. The impact is simple. There is hardly any time for the peace in mind.

The recent trend for senior management individuals has been to opt for an annual break of 15 to 20 days to unwind but what about the daily course of life? I am in sync with the opinion that if we continuously think of work-related issues and keep ourselves glued to the work premises, the quality is likely to get negatively impacted. This can be very well observed in a meeting which has stretched too long and the attendees keep gazing at their watches. While they might be physically present in the board room, they are mentally far away from the meeting context which ultimately impacts the meeting outcomes. One may be well-off in terms of earnings and luxuries of life but that does not ensure peace of mind resulting in irritation, frustrations and creating an environment of unhappiness. Bringing work life balance to all individuals is one of the prime responsibilities of an organizational head.

I recollect an instance in my career when I was with Bhilai Steel Plant. We were involved at the steel melting shop for TQM related activities. The executives, as a routine manner, used to leave their workplace not before 7 to 7.30 pm where ideally, they should have left by 5.30pm. The major reason for this behaviour was since their boss preferred sitting late, they could not take the liberty to leave on time which apparently would give the notion to their boss that they are leaving early. A few months later there was a change in leadership and the new incumbent, after a couple of days, wanted to know as to why the staff members were overstaying at the office? He was anxious to know if they did not require any rest or feel the need to devote time to their family members. Then came one fine day when he made an announcement that any overstay beyond the working hours would attract an adverse remark in an individual's confidential report. Everyone started to leave on time and as expected, there was no negative impact either on productivity or on quality. This is what leadership is supposed to be, caring for people obviously building a sense of respect for the leader.

People Involvement Vs. Engagement

'People Involvement' has been listed as one among the 14 management principles of Dr. Edward Deming. This is a significant and an essential parameter for all day-to-day operational as well as functional activities in order to achieve better outputs, minimizing the variance between the indices of plan against actuals.

In today's business scenario, employees in addition to their routine jobs must be engaged in various improvement initiatives for better performance. These engagements would not only improve operational metrics but will boost the morale of employees and in turn the employees will also ensure that they deliver their best. The improvement initiatives may be TQM, 5S, Kaizen, Lean Manufacturing, TPM, Kanban and many more.

Listed below are a few attributes of an engaged employee:

1. Qualities of Engaged Employees:
   a. Believe in their organization
   b. Have the desire and work to change things for better
   c. Understand the bigger picture in business context

d. Respect and help co-workers whenever needed
e. Willing to take extra responsibility

2. Salient Features of Engaged Employees:
    a. Credible leadership
    b. Supportive co-workers
    c. Job and career satisfaction
    d. High performing organization
    e. Committed employees
    f. Satisfied and loyal customers
    g. High performing workforce
    h. Productive and profitable organization

Observations made by Gallup Inc, an American management consulting company reveals that only 32% of employees are reported being engaged i.e. enthusiastic and committed to work where as 68% employees don't feel engaged at their work places out of which 16% have expressed their unhappiness most of the times and do not support their colleagues to do better thus tagging themselves to the band commonly referred as 'actively disengaged employees'.

One can thus conclude that improvements do not happen automatically. They need to be done with extra efforts at the senior management level. Only actively engaged employees will contribute towards sustainable improvements.

Self-Appraisal

Let me share a citation I recently came across in LinkedIn. I realized and learnt a lot and would like to encourage employed people to know, learn and start practicing, instead of waiting for half-yearly or yearly appraisals:

A little boy went to a telephone booth which was at the cash counter of a store and dialled a number. The storeowner observed and listened to the conversation:

Boy: *'Madam, can you give me the job of cutting your lawn?'*

Woman: *(at the other end of the phone line) 'I already have someone to cut my lawn.'*

Boy: *'Madam, I will cut your lawn for half the price than the person who cuts your lawn now.'*

Woman: *'I'm very satisfied with the person who is presently cutting the lawn.'*

Boy: *(with more perseverance) 'Madam, I'll even sweep the floor and the stairs of your house for free.'*

Woman: *'No, thank you.'*

With a smile on his face, the little boy put the receiver down. The store owner, who was listening to all this, walked over to the boy.

Storeowner: *'Son, I like your attitude; I like that positive spirit and would like to offer you a job.'*

Boy: *'No thanks.'*

Storeowner: *'But you were really pleading for one.'*

Boy: *'No Sir, I was just checking my performance at the job I already have. I am the one who is working for that lady I was talking to!'*

This is called 'Self-Appraisal'. Give your best and the world comes to you.

Don't relax or display a lazy attitude as the whole world is watching you. In the Gita, Lord Krishna says, 'If you don't fight for what you want, don't cry for what you have lost'. Nothing depends on luck; everything depends on work because even luck has to work. These are powerful verses and let us practice them in our lives.

Decision Making - Within and Beyond Our Control

I recollect the teaching of one of my school teachers, Dr. Manrakhan Lal Sahu, during my days at Bhilai. During one of his Hindi classes, he had once asked us to underline a sentence that read as 'Suno Sabki, Karo Apni' meaning 'Listen to all but act on your own'. He spent sufficient time in explaining to us the significance of the text and emphasized that we adhere to it throughout our life. He further added that it may not be important from an examination point of view but would prove to be of immense importance in our practical life. He explained that whenever we had to decide, we must involve all concerned to obtain different views on the subject matter thereby analysing the probability of impact of all the views that were expressed. However, the final decision should always rest on us and should be made by us which we internally feel is the one that really adds value.

Let me also cite another lesson of my life that made me learn to become bold in decision making. This happened during the days when I was associated with projects at Bhilai. It was a Saturday when I and an engineer in-charge of M/s Hindustan Steelworks Construction Limited (HSCL) were standing near a cable tunnel that was getting ready for concreting. I observed that a portion of the tunnel for which approval was sought, was a middle portion and there was a gap of 100mm once the two adjoining parts were placed on either end. I knew that the gap was neither going to impact the laying of cable pipes nor the functioning of the cables, but since the finishing in terms of the gap was not matching with the drawing, I told the engineer that I would hold my decision of approving the job. As the next day was a Sunday, I apprised him that the earliest I could revert to him was Monday after I had consulted our appointed designers, M/s Metallurgical & Engineering Consultants Limited (MECON). The engineer repeatedly requested me to approve the job in order that he could meet his timelines and targets.

On my denial, the engineer approached the then Additional Chief Engineer Mr. N V Krishnamurthy (If I recollect correctly) with the matter. I was at the job site when I suddenly realized a hand resting on my right shoulder. To my surprise, it was Mr. Krishnamurthy. He asked me how the things were going and then raised the matter and enquired whether the gap would affect the functioning of the cable to which I replied that it would not. He asked me what the issue was in approving the job. He insisted that the approval would also assist our own job progress targets being met. I replied by saying that I would need clearance from MECON before approving the job. My boss added that if I was clear about the result, I could approve the job the same day insisting that MECON would provide the clearance after listening to my verbatim. He further added that in case of an unlikely event he would take the responsibility of any adverse consequences.

I got convinced and approved the job. As per plan I went to MECON office on Monday at Ispat Bhavan and explained the matter. To my surprise the engineer looked at me and said, 'if you are convinced', I am convinced too and signed and gave their clearance under their official stamp. The resolution of the entire matter at MECON took at most two to three minutes for which I was hesitant in giving a decision on Saturday. I returned happily and realized the significance of making a bold decision. I still remember my boss and continue to enjoy his great lesson even today.

So, my takeaway would be to learn how to decide. If you are convinced with your decision, in 90% cases, it would be a right decision and in case of the balance 10% when you get to learn that it was a wrong decision, invest your efforts to know what would have been the right decision. Practical learning should be our lifetime agenda. So, dare to take decision in line with Welspun's beautiful Quote 'Dare to commit'.

The two instances cited above proved helpful during many occasions in my career. Many times, it may so happen that a few members will not agree with your decision but if you are confident of your thoughtful decision, then please go ahead as in 90% cases it would be the correct decision. My heartfelt respect to both the seniors, wherever they are today. A blockbuster Bollywood movie has quoted '

जो डर गया, समझो मर गया. So, it is time that we need to decide whether we are here to live or to die. I believe that we are here not only to live but also to make others live too. If you are in sync with this belief, then please join me.

Truth and Spirituality

Many management gurus have repeatedly mentioned that all decisions we make should be based on analysed data and data should be based on facts. It means that whatever we do at professional and personal levels, it should be connected to truth. The same also applies to the way we called ourselves as human but the element of 'being human', that is 'being kind to human' is missing among many of us.

I am a believer of the traits such as 'Truth, Honesty, Being Human and Believing in Supreme Power' are directly or indirectly linked to spirituality. I take this opportunity to thank Bollywood actor Mr. Salman Khan for owning and overseeing his charitable organization that has been extending support to the needy since 2007. Thank you Mr. Salman!

Key Take Away:

No one succeeds alone. It does not matter how big or small your dream is; being successful is never a single man's effort. Einstein had Max Talmud, his mentor. Mozart has his father, Leopold. A company has its employees, an entrepreneur has associates, a manager has colleagues, so on and so forth. The team is as essential as the self in realizing the success story. You can only reach the tip of the iceberg when you have a broad-base foundation to support the iceberg.

The team is an extension of the self, and just like the self it needs to be regularly assessed, trained, developed and disciplined. Learning is an ongoing process and one can never be too old to learn. Knowledge and skill development are key steps towards success. The team and the self must constantly be exposed to new learning to achieve improvement through regular assessment and discipline. The zeal and determination to learn make a leader stand out from the crowd. But it is not mindless slogging that makes a leader. A successful leader knows how to work in temperance – how to strike that essential balance between work and home. After all, all work and no play does make Jack a dull boy.

'Coming together is a beginning, staying together is progress, and working together is success.'

– Henry Ford

Chapter 9

Targeting Zero Defect and Zero Effect

Based on my long and rich experience across diverse industry segments, I believe that Zero Defect for every delivery and Zero Effect in surroundings is possible. The guiding principle to achieve this would be to follow what I had mentioned earlier of 'Doing right things right, first time and every time'. This must be followed and practised by everyone across the workforce chain, beginning right from the top management till the lowest level.

An integrated management system needs to be developed with a daily Gemba round by all stakeholders, an all-round training on need-based skills encompassing technical, management systems, behavioural to facilitate and empower the performer to discharge his/her duties that target zero-defect outputs. The management has to ensure that motivational systems are in place, viz. unhealthy workplace dynamics, especially at senior level are avoided and not encouraged, celebrations are made a habit, appreciations are conveyed in public whereas criticism is made only in a one-to-one forum, which are some of the good practices that are set right. A carrot in one hand and stick in the other approach to counselling has to be intelligently and sensitively enforced wherein an extraordinary performance is rewarded and a lagging performance should be first conveyed and support should be extended for gearing up and even after that if an improvement is not noticed only then should be taken to tasks.

Planning is very crucial in designing the 'overall tension-free management system'. In fact, to achieve zero-defect deliveries, we need to develop zero-defect processes and it needs enough time. Once an effective management system is developed, the top management only needs to monitor on-line and obtain updates from immediate subordinates about the progress but need to be constantly cautious that those in confidence do not take undue advantage of misleading or spreading misconception in the working environment.

Once this process has been established the top management may very well devote their valuable time for future businesses. It may be noted that all reputed organizations in existence for years follow these types of management systems and hence are able to sustain their leadership worldwide.

The Paradigm Shift: From Correction to Prevention

A focus towards reduction in rejection and rework is a mandatory compliance when it comes to promoting a profitable culture in an organization. Seiichi Nakajima San, the founder member of TPM, emphasized on designing equipment which simply could not lead to a defect. In line with the same analogy of TPM, is it not possible to design and develop an effective management system including a decision-making process that can never have a flaw. To make it simple, let us understand the following terminologies of quality management.

Correction:

Eliminating existing non-conformity i.e. repairing, re-processing, re-grading.

Benefit: Reduces or eliminates harmful effects

Corrective Action:

Eliminating cause of existing non- conformity

Benefit: Prevents recurrence

Preventive Action:

Eliminating cause of potential non-conformity

Benefit: Prevents occurrence

The Corrective Action requires one to perform a Why-Why Analysis on 4Ms (Man, Machine, Material, Method) and E (Environment). For instances wherein there are many causes, a balanced approach in line with the 80-20 Pareto Analysis needs to be adopted. One needs to be careful that fact-based correct data is picked and the analysis is carried out with patience; else the whole exercise would be a waste of time and effort. More significantly, such an incorrectly conducted exercise will fetch a wrong conclusion and mislead the organization which might prove both costly and futile.

The Preventive Action requires one to perform a PFMEA (Process Failure Modes & Effects Analysis) by adopting a cross-functional approach. For further details, one can refer to IATF 16949:2016, an International Standard for Automotive Quality Management Systems jointly developed by IATF (International Automotive Task Force) Members and approved and published by ISO (International Organization for Standardization).

'You won't get anything more if you don't do more. Same actions breed the same results. Raise your standards and work ethic; then anything is possible'.

Synchronize Your Improvement Initiatives

Organizations these days run many parallel initiatives in their attempt towards aiming for rapid development. Often most of such initiatives are reactive rather than being proactive. There is no harm as at least the initiatives have been rolled out. However, in order to achieve effective outcomes, it is necessary that such initiatives be synchronized. One must consider the fact that the workforce implementing these initiatives are the same resources who are engrossed in their routine daily work and meeting their assigned targets which is also the foremost necessity of the management.

Synchronization of these initiatives is what an organization should look out for in order that the initiatives are centrally aligned under the supervision of the top management. A positive reinforcement to this aspect in present times has been the clubbing of all ISO standards, QMS, safety and environment-related audits and their simultaneous implementation. This improves the effectiveness coupled with a reduction in cost. One of the initiatives of the government has been the emphasis on Lean Manufacturing Practices which encompasses all good initiatives that are available today. The implementation of Standard Operating Procedures (SOP) related to quality, safety 5S, Total Productive Maintenance (TPM) (either all or few selected pillars), Inspection Test Plan (ITP) and Inspection Test Records (ITR) and their associated benefits are an example of good initiatives triggered by lean manufacturing practices. Quality Council of India (QCI) and Ministry of Industries have made commendable contributions in this aspect. While a lot of MSMEs have started reaping the benefits, for some the process has been slow owing to the delay made by them to get convinced in implementing the above good initiatives.

The ideation for adoption of new initiatives is necessary to meet and beat competition; but synchronization of the initiatives is a must after thoughtful discussions. The workforce or the team who will execute the implementation should not be left to wander in the thought process of ambiguity, lack of clarity and decision making. A better way would also be to empower the stakeholders who are responsible for productivity and quality to simultaneously drive, monitor and own these initiatives.

Avoiding Work Politics

Our workplace is a setup where individuals from diverse backgrounds, different educational qualifications and varied interests come together to work towards a common organizational goal. The success and failure of an organization are directly proportional to the amount of hard work put by each employee. Individuals must work as a single unit to avoid unnecessary conflicts and politics at the workplace. An individual must treat his organization as a priority. A sense of belongingness and dedication towards work is important. It is essential for the employees to work together in close coordination with each other to deliver their level best. A sense of unity is important to extract the best out of the employees. Transparency must be maintained at all levels for a positive ambience at the workplace.

Office politics arises when employees tend to misuse their power to gain undue attention and popularity at the workplace. Employees indulge in work politics simply to tarnish their colleague's reputation, to obtain advantages and find place in the good books of their superiors. A few reasons for office politics are listed below:

a. Employees aspiring to come in the limelight without much hard work, depend on politics.

b. Politics arises when employees aspire to achieve something beyond their authority and control in a short span of time.

c. Lack of supervision and control at the workplace.

d. Too much gossip at work leads to politics.

e. Arrogant superiors

f. Jealous colleagues

These might be a few reasons for the inception, nurturing and growth of this unwanted parameter. One of the foremost I feel is having too many heads at the top level. The lack of clarity or overlapping of individual responsibilities and authorities also fuel politics at workplace. While some individuals may have a direct approach or may be close to entrepreneurs, a few individuals who possess extraordinary talent or high qualifications and are really masters in their domain but lack in behavioural skills generally are inclined to make their own group within the organization. Such individuals are conscious about their 2 Ps – Power and Package - and normally don't stick to one place for a longer duration. And once he leaves, the new person starts with a different approach, leaving the workforce in dilemma thereby slowing down progress. To be successful in his new endeavour, the new person needs to understand the history of the organization, the culture, identify the positive employees in the group, calibrate his/her own ideas and own acceptability at the new place and then proceed further.

My suggestion would be to also conduct a psychological test by a third party during the recruitment of middle and higher-level executives. This might help in understanding their soft skills in a better way. It may be noted that big names in the market may not be big on their soft skills. On several occasions, it has been observed that a junior level person may try to take senior executives into confidence by conveying wrong information about someone for a wrong intention and try to tarnish his good image. This may be a result of a feeling of grudge of some past occasion when the individual might have been criticized or pulled up for his lagging performance. The problem aggravates when the recipient of such false information is weak on his ears and is unable to ascertain the authenticity of the information received and start believing it.

The silent workers normally have high esteem and get demotivated very easily by any unexpected behavioural pattern of their superiors and start looking for another job which is a loss to the organization. An organization with a high turnover may sometimes not bother about such employee concerns. There are exceptions too where the management does listen to the negative talks about someone but doesn't blindly believe in whatever is being said because true leaders know what to accept from whom and what to ignore. Such leaders ensure that employees enter office with a positive state of mind and leave their ego at the doorstep.

Key Take Away:

Spearheaded by the current Prime Minister Narendra Modi, Zero Defect Zero Effect was started off as a slogan that favourably went on to become a program that can be easily adopted towards a greater goal. It may have started as a program to promote industries that do not have defects and have no effect on the environment, but one can easily adopt this practice at work and for the self too.

Perfection and improvement are integral to success. While most agree that failures and imperfections are part of the process of achieving perfection, one can't deny the active effort that needs to be put in order to avoid failures and imperfections. Striving from the beginning under the guidance of good leaders to achieve something without defect is of utmost importance. The old habit of bypassing even one defect or one flaw needs to be put to an end now. Prevention is better than cure – both in production processes and in one's life situations. The sooner one adopts this stance, the faster one will reduce defects and effects. When a determined single focused effort is channelled towards a bigger goal, the risk of being distracted by petty ancillary things gets eliminated – a possibility only when a good leader steps up to resourcefully and harmoniously bind a good team. Improvement and growth eventually lead you to success, instead of failures that gets caught up in correction.

'Treatment without prevention is simply unsustainable.'

- Bill Gates

Chapter 10

Unwind and Relax...No Tension!

Stress is not always bad. In fact, a little amount of stress is necessary to achieve our goals. Stress is derived from the Latin word 'stringere' meaning to stay tight or compressed. Stress is good but needs to be managed properly and is worst if it cannot be managed well. It is a gap between expectation and reality and the more is the gap the greater is the stress. Stress is often associated with the past whereas the future brings in anxiety.

Stress can be reduced by planning our work that we are capable of and accomplishing them within the committed timeframe. A limited stretch of the target without compromising the aspect of practicality of achieving the stretched target will lead to improved performance. Care should be taken that such stretches do not lead to a person becoming a workaholic. Stress buster activities like going out for a walk, enjoying a movie, visiting a restaurant, spending time with family and friends should be a part of daily life and should never be compromised.

Medication must be planned to be replaced by meditation. An association for a social cause can also assist one to have one's mind get diverted from regular monotonous work routine. However, care should be taken that such social associations should not be associated with politics and if the same is sensed one should at once refrain from associating oneself with such initiatives. Music, either vocal or instrumental, has always relaxed the human mind. Adopting animals may also give peace of mind to many individuals both by a sense of satisfaction of providing a shelter to helpless creature and by developing a new loyal companion in one's daily life. Even the Almighty shall be pleased by this benevolent act.

Some of the suggestions to keep you relaxed:

- Start your morning every day by listening to some bhajans, Sufi songs, meditational or any good instrumental music depending on individual liking.

- Saying good morning with genuine smiles to everyone starting from family members, people you meet on the way or to your driver, all colleagues especially the junior staff/ workers, etc. You may also ask security/cleaning staff of your residential societies as 'कैसे हो? सब ठीक है?' etc.

- In case someone greets you with a good morning, you may reply as very good morning.

- Fix a time for WhatsApp, just to look at any important message, reply can be given on the way, if convenient ... since this is becoming a disease day by day.

  We should use the good part of technology suiting to our requirements rather than be led by it.

  Avoid commenting on political/religious messages, if you can reserve it. Because the moment you reply at least a few messages will be contradicting your thinking which you may not like, causing stress.

- At least once or twice in a month, if not possible every week, go for a day outing or to see movies in cinema halls or restaurants. In the hall while viewing movies, have a bucket of popcorns to your taste, salty or cheese or caramel, and enjoy with your family members and experience the magic of tension getting released at minimal cost. 100% guarantee in comparison to star hotels. If you are in PVR you may get complimentary also. I am mentioning since we enjoy at our Orion Mall at Panvel. Sometimes you may bring some unique dish packed while returning home.

- At night, please watch some entertaining competitions like Indian Idol in Sony, SaReGaMaPa in Zee in Hindi or regional channels, dance competitions like Dance + by Remo D'Souza, India Got Talent etc.
- Episodes that help release tensions are laughter shows in various channels especially Kapil Sharma show etc.
- One of the value-adding show is 'Kaun Banega Crorepati' which is entertainment plus knowledge. Hats off to Amitabhjee – the way he conducts is simply superb! And of course, the production team.
- Another way of reducing stress, what I have adopted, is minimal watching of political debates on TV shows because in the end you don't come out with some concrete conclusion or direction, but with more irritation.

The above shows one or the other not only will act as a stress buster but also enhance our knowledge about different cultures. We must appreciate the new talents struggling their way to get to the top on these shows. It may so happen that some of us get motivated; that's again one of the benefits of technology.

Another activity which I have started recently and getting instant benefit is that I have stopped watching so-called 'debates in TV Channels. Having a little bit of leadership quality and being quite sensitive in societal and national issues, I used to get tensed but after watching couple of years I realized that there is no conclusion; neither we could do anything. I have written what I am doing; in your case you may make your own choice. However, I feel relaxed on reading latest reports analysis which we can see next day in newspapers.

Tips for Overcoming Mental Fatigue

We all require regular periods of silence and solitude in our lives in the midst of a fast-paced lifestyle. Our days are busy where most of us have a lot of actions to perform. So, would I like to have a mind which is filled completely with thoughts or do I like it with fewer thoughts and greater spaces between them? Our emotional carriers are our minds which carry the weight of our thoughts. The fewer the thoughts and the lighter they are, and the minds will be always enthusiastic.

Let's look at the following five techniques to keep our minds flying in joy always:

1. ***Create one thought at a time ~***

   An anxious mind having full of fear thinks excessively and faster than what is required and sometimes creates false future realities.

2. ***Think of others only when necessary ~***

   A common habit that we all have is to think of others even when it is not necessary and important. We, therefore, get tired and experience mental fatigue.

3. ***Give up your ego and live freely ~***

   A very heavy weight that some of us are carrying on our heads is of our subtle ego. We need to practice being humble, kind and not to mind other people's comments. Think of bowing down and the excessive thoughts of feeling insulted will stop. It will keep our minds light.

4. ***Take a pledge … Life is a light Journey, not a burdensome one ~***

   A very important practice for experiencing life without getting burdened is to enjoy the journey.

5. ***Your thoughts create your realities ~***

   Be your own Monitor; this is an extremely important and vital aspect of keeping your thoughts less in number, very positive and light, in order to remain free from mental fatigue.

Rest, Refresh, and Rejuvenate Your Mind

It is said that about 40,000 to 50,000 thoughts are generated each day. Many of these thoughts are negative or wasteful, and this makes our mind tired. This makes it hard for us to focus, to find the right words or to stay positive. Hence, we need to slow down the constant stream of thoughts arising in our mind.

Following steps may be followed to rest, refresh and rejuvenate minds:

1. Every morning, thank your mind for managing everything - your body, relationships and work.
2. Nourish it with 15/20 minutes of meditation, read content that reinforce peace and happiness.
3. Create and visualize an affirmation of how you want your day to be.

4. At work, focus only on the positives in people and situations.
5. Pause for one minute after every hour to relax and clean your mind of any negativity.
6. Meditate at bedtime and resolve any issue in the mind, for a good night's sleep.

Repeat these affirmations three times a day to create a relationship with your mind and cleansing it regularly.

"I am a powerful being … I take care of my mind … I meditate every morning for 20 minutes … I create my affirmation … I visualize my day being and doing what I want … I study for 20 minutes … I respond right to every situation … I avoid negative information from media, social media and people … I pause for a minute every hour … to rest my mind … I meditate before I go to bed… It charges my mind"

When we take charge of our thoughts and start regulating them, our mind naturally slows down and thinks right in every situation. Taking care of our mind is the first step in taking care of people and situations.

Love Animals

Animals are innocent and one among them is a dog. Dogs are the most loyal **creatures** in the world. I have not heard of them betraying anyone. They rather help us in identifying the culprits of any bad incidents. Their intelligent and brave skills have been used by bomb detection squads, police, military; and they have even left their footprint of contribution is space and research. We all are aware of their bravery and loyalty, yet when it comes to daily life many of us hate, beat and even torture them, portraying how cruel and selfish we can be.

You must have read in newspapers:

a. A dog was thrown on the ground/road from the roof top of a high-rise building

b. A cat was thrown out from the 16th floor

c. A few years back while playing on the top of a society, children put crackers around the tail of a dog, staying in the society for many years. Naturally after a few seconds, it jumped from the roof.

These are only a few examples to share. In all the above cases, these innocent animals met with multiple fractures and ultimately died.

These animals are innocent; they need a little bit of food and love from us. In the third case, the dog died only after the family who used to feed him came back and started looking for it. The dog noticed that they came back and after hearing their voice it crawled to the point where they stood and died silently. It's eyes were sending a message ' look at what they did to me'. Are we human beings? For security reasons we need them but what treatment are we giving to them?

Through this book, I request each of my dear readers to start loving animals and contribute to their well-being by at least providing the leftover food of your homes and spread the same message across your neighbourhood.

It has been well established that if you have an animal in your house, you should take care of them well and really love them; they help in reducing your tensions to a maximum extent!

We also need to think of having adequate number of crematoriums for animals in different locations; this will not only give you peace of mind but also help in maintaining a hygienic environment.

Tel Aviv has the largest number of cemeteries for dogs in the world. It even has dog parks, dog beaches and fountains for thirsty canines.

How many of us bring a dog out of love and affection, but mostly for security purposes. Can we think of picking up puppies from the road to provide them shelter!

But the problem is that a few of us are quite selfish by nature. The moment a dog starts suffering from any disease, we try to leave them alone in an unknown area; this is really a torture to them which these innocents are unable to convey.

Similarly, we try to take out maximum possible quantity of milk from cows/buffaloes and when they are not in a condition to serve us because of age factor, we leave them on the road on their own or even sell them to unwanted agencies. Will we be behaving in the same manner with our relatives? Please think!

Make Celebration a Habit

The word 'Celebration' itself brings energy with it. The trend to celebrate has of late been picking up fast in most of the organizations. Celebration in an organization gives a homely touch in the minds of employees at all levels. Cohesiveness and the spirit of team building get enhanced. The best way is to celebrate for every small achievement instead of waiting for something big to happen. One should always plan to celebrate birthdays, good kaizens, accident-free days in a month, getting awards from third parties, festivals, milestones of service period, appreciations from suppliers and even customers, successful third-party assessments, picnics, foundation day, etc. The event irrespective of their size should be designed in such a way that employees instead of going home or somewhere outside for spending some enjoyable moments are able to live those moments in their own workplace.

Key Take Away:

The old adage, 'All work and no play makes Jack a dull boy' are golden words that still hold true no matter how far we have progressed or how adept we are at dealing with life. A dull boy is hardly ever able to contribute to betterment or greatness. A dull boy who is mentally, physically and emotionally fatigued is struggling more to sustain any semblance of life, than to make the most of the available resources and make or do something brilliant out of it. Gone are the days of stretching from one limb to the other, until you can't stretch anymore, and eventually become a zombie that works daily on set patterns – patterns that are old, growing redundant over time and would soon become obsolete.

Be the bright girl who knows the importance of balancing work and play at the same time. Be the bright insightful person who knows where to take a breath and navigate between work and home without jeopardizing one for the other. A productive brain with innovative ideas and a determined zeal can only survive when you let it breathe and play in the space away from stress, tension and stagnancy. It is foolhardy to not realize that even working like a robot without proper breaks or without annihilating stress, one is almost akin to rotting in stagnant water; and stagnant water breeds no fresh life.

'Adopting the right attitude can convert negative stress into a positive one.'

-Hans Selye

Chapter 11

Be an Effective and Efficient Value Adder

Effectiveness is about 'DOING THINGS RIGHT, FIRST-TIME, EVERY TIME'. The concept of 'Zero Defect Deliveries'.

EFFICIENCY is all about how fast the 'Zero Defect Materials and Services' can be delivered. It is about the SPEED.

In the fast-paced modern competitive world, there will always be a demand for EFFECTIVE and EFFICIENT resources. So, it is left to you to decide whether you would want to be recognized and valued differently or you are contended to continue your approach of being 'A face in the crowd'.

Essential Habits

In addition to Stephen R Covey's habits of highly effective people, I feel the following sixteen habits which are essential to work at ground level in achieving success and thereby leading a comfortable and happy life and should be practiced by every individual.

1. Macro Planning- Yearly/Six Monthly/Quarterly
2. Micro Planning- Monthly/Daily
3. Work Prioritization… Official/Personal
4. Time Management (Valuable)
5. True to Yourself
6. Be Vocal … Support Right & Highlight Wrong
7. Identify & Understand Customer Requirements
8. Respect Systems & Instructions at Site
9. Seek Suggestions but Take Your Own Decision
10. Respect for Other's Views
11. Sticking to Commitments
12. Attending meetings with updated status & data
13. Understand Your Scope of Work/Responsibilities
14. Communication …. Effective & Efficient
15. Seek Candid Feedback & Improve
16. Golden Rule

Daily Work Management (DWM)

There must be a dedicated effort to ensure a continuously increasing level of quality in the deliveries we make. Such an effort is necessary to retain the attention of the customers for repeat business. In a way it is an integrated organizational approach directed towards customer delight, involving everyone, using problem-solving methodologies and continually improving products, processes and services.

The degree of success depends on how we can internalize and develop a close monitoring system to find out the current status of progress. If everything is going as planned, people should be motivated to think other methods of working, so that they do still better than what they are currently doing. And in the adverse case where targets could not be achieved, the focus should be on why it could not happen thereby initiating corrective measures for such failures. We can't wait till a considerable time gets elapsed and then know the status.

It is for these reasons that we need to establish a system of Daily Work Management including walking around the work premises in full or part. Once the walk is over, the respective stakeholders should assemble at a predetermined place for a short informal meeting to understand progress of the previous day on indicators of Productivity (P), Quality (Q), Cost (C), Delivery (D), Safety (S) and Morale (M) commonly referred as the 'PQCDSM' parameters, starting with safety statistics and prioritizing the day's schedule. In this way we know what exactly is needed to be done within the next 24 hrs. An ideal way would be to start the meeting with a prayer, thanking the Almighty for the good things that happened and seeking blessings for rest of the day.

I believe that leadership is needed at workplace somewhat in line with the 'Gemba concept. (Gemba is a Japanese term meaning 'the real place'). This is necessary to cut short the decision-making process by enabling fact-based right and quick decision at the right time. Such decisions will always be based on the interaction with people at the work site involving all levels of workers understanding their genuine problems and in turn guide and motivate them as after all the quality is built by them. Once all of us together with a unified approach can do these simple things, the world will be ours.

Making Continual Improvement a habit

I heard from a video being circulated where Mr. Rajeev of Bajaj Group narrates about the initial conversation that took place between him and Mr. Yamaguchi, the TPM guru.

Thanks to Mr. Rajeev for sharing for the benefit of the Senior Management Team.

During the conversation about Mr. Yamaguchi, he asks all senior management executives what their responsibilities were. The replies were … 'I am so and so …., head of …… on design front'

He asks are you involved in designing …. No, then…. looking after operations, ok … so you are operating machines… no… no I am In- charge but what you are doing, I am taking care of customers ok, so you are marketing the products or taking care of customer care …no … no, I am the overall in- charge. It means you don't do anything only giving instructions … or conducting meetings.

It is really a shocking question and may be addressed to most of senior management team.

Mr. Yamaguchi told Mr Rajeev that Continual Improvement in every function, every department, every process, every machine, every system across the organization, on all the days is the main responsibility of Senior Management Team!

Can we ask ourselves 'where do we stand on the above'?

What the TPM Guru perhaps wanted to refer about kaizen … doing good for better every moment. Many bosses set a target of kaizens for employees and if not given they are fired back; perhaps the essence has not been understood well by them.

Key Take Away:

Remember, to succeed …
Dress smartly
Behave decently
Talk softly
Work patiently
Think creatively
Earn honestly
Act fearlessly
Have work life balance

Maintain meeting etiquette as given below:
Attend with preparations
Stay in meeting
Mobile in silent mode
Stick to the subject & be brief
Avoid side conversation
Avoid interruptions
Support right decisions, which are in favour of organization
Attend with a diary for follow up
Make own minutes, don't wait for official release of minutes

Because becoming successful is your own responsibility!

Chapter 12

Social and National Responsibility

'No success or achievement in material terms is worthwhile unless it serves the needs or interests of the country and its people and is achieved by fair & honest means.'

-JRD Tata

Shri JRD Tata said the above lines many years back, but the same is still being followed and preserved as a culture by the group as a legacy. By now we are all aware of what the TATA Sons have done under the leadership of Shri Ratan Tata for the 26/11 terror struck victims of Mumbai. An excellent example of Corporate Responsibility!

I have known a little bit about Tata Nagar (Jamshedpur) culture since my childhood. They don't do things just for the sake of doing. Neither do they do for public applause or for getting few relaxations from the government. I once met Shri Ratan Tata at a seminar at Taj Lands End due to courtesy of my friend, Rajendra Potdar. I was on the second row eagerly waiting to see him in person. He entered and passed by me but to my surprise he looked at me and asked through his body language, 'How are you?'. I replied, 'Thank You Sir' but forgot to say 'Fine'. He smiled and moved ahead. I was mesmerized by his personality. So humble and down to earth. He patiently attended the programme for about three hours. Many attendees took the advantage of meeting and shaking hands with him. I could barely notice any level of ego in him as he was walking around and meeting people.

After my silent acquaintance with him during his entry, I

dared to meet him once again as he was about to leave. I must have crossed many people with the speed of an express train and somehow got to place myself in front of him. I frankly told him that I missed to shake hands with him. The tall gentleman humbly extended his hand in between the crowd and shook hands with me. A dream came true for me and I was indebted for the moment. As was expected, a few people started asking me if Shri Ratan Tata knew me. I could not refrain from taking the apparent honour of not knowing him and replied that yes, he did but it had been a long time since we met. My response could pacify the query of the person who then made his way to the food table.

I have no knowledge as to how good Shri Ratan Tata gets his sleep, but one thing was sure that I could not sleep well due to anxiety. It must be that he found my face familiar as if he had known me before.

'None can destroy iron, but its OWN RUST can!' - Ratan Tata

Shri Azim Premji of Wipro Group is another personality I have great respect for. To me, he has contributed a lot in terms of spreading education to villages. I had the honour of witnessing him once accepting an award from Institute of Directors at a hotel in Mumbai.

'One of the pre-requisites for children becoming proactive and responsible citizens is the availability of enough role models inside and outside the school.'

- Azim Premji

It is rightly said that until you spread your wings, you will have no idea how far you can fly.

Key Take Away:

The ones with a myopic view will consider success as a personal goal – a personal task that one has achieved. It is in fact far from being personal or achieved in isolation. With success comes power, and with power comes responsibility. A truly successful person, who has grown both personally and professionally, will know that success is never a personal agenda. It never lies singularly and is detached from everyone else around you. In fact, it connects you to hundred other people who depend on your success for betterment, improvement and opportunities. You may be one of those few who have been able to carve out your road to success like a true leader, but as a true leader one must also realize the responsibility it brings to take care of the ones who have no access to privilege and give back to those who have assisted you in reaching the zenith. A true leader gives back ten times more of what was taken from the society and people. A true leader realizes the importance of assisting to help create more leaders for a better world.

Your Notes/What do I need to clarify from the Author

May please approach the author at:
sapan_bardhan@rediffmail.com

Chapter 13

Be a True Human Being

It's easy to say that we should be a true human being but needs tremendous efforts and time as well, one of the hurdles may be our own ego. Better to listen to our inner conscience. Experts say the true self inside does not support wrong doings, but we overlook what comes from within.

In my personal experience, thinking good for others, extending support wherever and whenever possible, trying one's best to make others happy is a good example of being human.

Being human to others including animals is more important than simply remain a human being.

I still remember, when I was heading the HR function, one of the senior most persons, really a nice person, was to retire after serving the organisation. I started thinking how to make his last day in the organisation more memorable for the rest of the life. The farewell ceremony as usual was supposed to be on the last day just before lunch time.

I wished to hand over the 'full and final settlement cheque' to this father-like person. At the outset, a few of the members said how is it possible, Sir? So many data required. I said stop other works and focus on collecting the required data, I also mentioned that the data we are supposed to have is within our department only. Team could not say anything, but someone said we can do it but what about accounts department to prepare the cheque on time. I replied 'that's my responsibility' and talked to head of accounts; he was kind enough to agree with the proposal.

Nobody other than the team of HR and one or two executives of accounts/ finance knew. We made this as a surprise. After all formalities, lectures, praises, bouquet etc it was just about to get over, I handed over the envelope to my boss who in turn gave it to Director for handing over to the retiring person. On declaring, it was a silence for few seconds and then clapping. First time in the history, full and final settlement cheque around 1.30/2.00 pm, although he was supposed to be in office till evening.

I still remember his face, a big smile, expression of surprise ? but highly satisfied person, with tears about to come out of his eyes!

Just before leaving office he visited my cabin, thanked and blessed me and my team!

A wonderful time in my life for what we did was nothing!

Just wanted to make him happy; in fact by doing so we all became happier.

Contrary to this, one unit head at Vadodara was to leave the organization, one head of a function who was administratively reporting to him, since not having good rapport with him made the ex-boss to come to his table, made him wait for some time and completed formalities as if doing a favour to him.

Surprisingly, he conveyed same to me with pride; I did not like his approach and told him categorically.

Don't misuse your power since you don't know till what time you will continue to enjoy the same status. I appreciate if you use your authority for doing good for the welfare of human beings and even for animals, the innocent ones.

Honour your own commitments

I have found that many persons who hold very high positions do not remember their appointments or commitment to someone for a meeting. At the scheduled time, when the person reaches their office they find out that the senior person is out of station and not available. On enquiring, the secretary showed inability to answer when he would be to meet next.

I believe this is one of the qualities senior management should have but if somebody forgets he would be getting a heavy firing for sure.

Once a Senior Person conveyed to me that he would be meeting on so and so date between X to Y Time. I was happy and prepared, but he did not come neither was there any message. On calling him on mobile he replied he is not well, rather he forgot also otherwise he could have conveyed and one word available for free is 'sorry ', we would certainly meet, when? would decide.

How can a member of senior management is unable to plan his own schedule ? In case of unavoidable situation, the same can be rescheduled.

Daily planning is part of overall planning. If you can't plan your own day and how do you expect the same from subordinates?

Purpose is not to criticise them but bringing out the fact and for them to avoid frustration and embarrassment.

Best thing is to use a monthly planner day- wise, time- wise to be adhered to, in case of a need, may change the date or time and convey the concerned person well before meeting time, thus getting a high regard. It's again a culture that we can lead by example.

Best part to learn from our ancient history 'the Golden Rule' you should behave with people as you would have expected from them. Problem here is by the virtue of having a higher post one learns to command without feeling any concern for the other person.

Key Take Away:

A success story is never an individual one, but it is also one that is steered by an individual. One can't stress enough on the importance that the team, the colleagues, one's family and society in general plays in making a person successful. These ingredients, if missing, will take a man only half-way on to the road of success.

But one can't also deny the agency that plays a role in carving one's road to success. Team, colleagues, family and society are at the disposal of hundreds and thousands of people. But only a few can climb on top of the ladder of success. Only few can make it out as the leader who has the ability and the capacity to take charge to man the ship, to guide the passengers on board it and to reach the end point. And though reaching the end point may be the goal of the journey, it is not the destination, but the journey that determines you as a true leader. A true leader, an honest successful man, is a sensitive, sensible and intelligent person who recognises the importance of human agency and situations above all else. A successful man who has experienced holistic growth will know the first step to being successful is to be a good human. Values, principles and morals have not come in existence to die. They still hold true, and in fact are of utmost importance to all successful people.

'Real success is not on the stage, but off the stage as a real human being, and how you get along with your fellow man.'

- Sammy Davis Jr.

Your Notes/What do I need to clarify from the Author

May please approach the author at:
sapan_bardhan@rediffmail.com

Chapter 14
Inspiring people

In today's scenario, the days have gone when you could order anyone around to get the things done to your choice or requirement. Even if they are working under you, they will be doing their jobs for the sake of doing without keeping quality or customer's satisfaction in mind.

So instead of ordering, we need to get their support by winning their hearts. Here the word motivation comes into picture. Motivation is all about getting people to act. But another great word is inspiration - making people inspired and to achieve this one has to exhibit/demonstrate leadership... the leadership by example.

For example, if you want everyone to report to duty on time, you yourself need to do so.

In a small scale company, the CEO wants everyone to enter the factory wearing safety shoes while he himself comes in chappals. The plant head shouts at employees if he finds anyone busy with WhatsApp on mobile; but in the office he not only remains busy with WhatsApp, he even makes people stand till he finishes reading the mobile messages.

Clarity in communication of 'what exactly is expected out of someone' and the reasons for the same helps in achieving what is needed and on time.

Treating employees as a family member helps in a long run; trust them, follow 'criticism in closed chamber and appreciation in open forum'. Be open to them … in case of losing a contract or missing a deadline which may call for penalty to the organisation. No employee would like that his company loses money or any good offer because people in general are good ... We need to only take out the best from them and that's why question of true leadership comes into picture.

In comparison to motivation, I feel 'Inspiration, involves changing the way people think and feel about themselves so that they want to take positive actions.

I would like to cite a real case .... in one of the small enterprise and factory which was loss making and lacked employee engagement. The company was struggling to overcome these losses. Company was just a 3 to 4-year-old unit. Management felt the need to change the style of working. MD and Owner handed over company to CEO. MD started one-to-one interaction with employees and started understanding his employees. He found that they are very much keen on educating their children. MD decided his company's vision - that "every employee's children will study in the best school and will make them highly educated "He volunteered to sponsor each child of employees who wants to pursue education/higher education. Every time he used to meet his employees, he used to ask about their kid's education. Thus the employees were inspired by the MD who considered that the company also belonged to them!

As employee engagement slowly improved, in a span of next one or two years the same company became profitable and now growing. Employees take pride in working for such a company.

Chapter 15

Making Life Beautiful

If we can accept the challenges of life like uncertainty, anxiety, apprehensions and fear, issues in relationship, suffering, ego, and can initiate a counter measure, our lives will change.

We have already discussed the following in previous chapters, few of the requisites for making life beautiful as per Sri Aurobindo Society are:

Faith in oneself
Courage
Perseverance
Humility
Generosity
Gratitude
Receptivity
Simplicity
Faith in almighty

'An inner life awakened to a full consciousness and to a full power of consciousness will bear its inevitable fruit in all who have it, self-knowledge, a perfected existence, the joy of a satisfied being, the happiness of a fulfilled nature'

- Sri Aurobindo

'Never grumble; all sorts of forces enter you when you grumble, and they pull you down. Keep smiling, a smile expresses the faith that nothing can stand against the Divine and that everything will come out all right in the end.'

- The Mother (Sri Aurobindo Society)

Happiness – the wrong beliefs and the truth

A significant number of people are suffering from depression in the world today. This is a hint for us to pause and ask if we are doing enough for our mental wellness, which is directly connected to emotional wellness. If we experience stress, anger, fear, hurt, jealousy, our emotional health suffers. Basically, we are caught in these negative emotions in pursuit of happiness. Most of us begin chasing dreams since childhood and do not pause thereafter for decades, because of the biggest incorrect belief that our happiness is what we acquire — that happiness is a by-product of our belongings. So, we seek happiness in accomplishments, possessions and relationships. Let us scrutinize these three popular but misleading beliefs.

Belief 1: Accomplishments make me happy.

Suppose I am an employee who knows that it takes two years to be promoted as a manager, I sincerely work for it. But my own conditioned thought often reminds me - I will be happy when promoted as a manager. So, I do not permit myself to be happy today, I will not permit for two more years. Some day if I sense that my promotion may not happen due to my inefficiency, or issues with team members or a management decision, I create stress, anger and anxiety since I believe these are not only affecting my career but snatching my happiness. I may resort to unfair means to get promotion. So, I create and transmit negativity, going into pain for two long years. If in this state I become a manager, can I be happy? Also, such happiness does not last as I will focus on the next promotion, then the next...

Truth: Happiness is not in our accomplishments. It is not to be postponed until our goal is reached. Happiness is in our way of thinking along the way, while working towards the goal.

Belief 2: I can buy happiness.

Suppose I believe that buying my dream car gives me happiness, I may purchase and own the most expensive car. I have essentially bought physical comfort. While on a long drive in it, I could get one phone call conveying unpleasant news which finishes my happiness. If my car gave happiness, happiness would stay despite the call. Even after the call, my car continues to give physical comfort and my physical body is comfortable. Since happiness is an emotional comfort, it disappeared when I (who was looking for happiness) went into pain after the call. Why do we feel happy upon buying a car? Because when we create a thought –

I bought my dream car - it generates a feeling of happiness. So, we used an object (car) as a stimulus to create a response (positive thought).

Truth: Let us not purchase objects seeking happiness in them. Everything physical is designed to give physical comfort. Happiness is an emotional comfort.

Belief 3: Family and friends give me happiness.

Oscillating between acceptance and expectations, our relationships are getting strained. We focus on what to get from relationships rather than give. The list of our expectations from each other are getting longer. We are accepting people only when they speak, behave according to our needs. If I equate my happiness to others obeying me, it cannot last. No sooner than someone obeys the first time, I hand out my next expectation. So, happiness leaves me at this point, only to return if the person obeys again. Else, I get upset. People have their definitions of rights and wrongs; so setting expectations will always hamper relationships and ruin happiness.

Truth: No one can make us happy or sad. Happiness is our emotion, our internal creation regardless of quality of our relationships.

Key Take Away:

A successful man is also a happy man. One must be really short sighted to think happiness come with money, comfort and luxury. One can have the riches of the world, but happiness can elude you even with a hefty bank account. Happiness can neither come with money, nor with power or with awards. Like a mirage that escapes and cheats the common eye, happiness can delude the common man into thinking that it can be bought or can be achieved with achievements and success.

A truly successful man will know that happiness is borne out of oneself. It cannot be produced, channelled or inspired. No one and nothing hold agency to our grief or our happiness. True happiness stems from within that is at peace. The fire of happiness is created by us, our own inner being. And this fire is also stroked by us – by our emotions, honesty and faith. Happiness lies not in the achievements but in the strive towards achievements. It is not so much the goal, but more the journey, the hard work and perseverance that will bring you happiness. Only a true leader will know that happiness is the goal that every successful man strives for.

'Success is not the key to happiness. Happiness is the key to success.'

- Albert Schweitze

Your Notes/What do I need to clarify from the Author

May please approach the author at:
sapan_bardhan@rediffmail.com

Chapter 16
Conquer the World

According to **Swami Vivekananda:**

'We are responsible for what we are and whatever we wish ourselves to be, we have the power to make ourselves. If what we are now has been the result of our past actions, it certainly follows that whatever we wish to be in future can be produced by our present actions, only we need to know how to act!'

This act depends upon our abilities. The ability to find the right ladder to climb upwards against the right wall at the right time with a right purpose, while having full grip on the ground assures you success. But the level or percentage of success depends entirely on the individual's abilities. The more we are spiritually awakened, the more success in terms of satisfaction and happiness can be observed.

Let us be optimistic that our future would be better than the past. We need to continue our efforts for betterment of the world - no retirement, no full stop! Here, I would like to mention again the universal law: what you give to others will one day come back to you. Be it - knowledge, help to the needy, motivation to others, a genuine smile, commitments or even hatred that will also come back to you one day or the other.

However, we need to make a habit of winning. If we do so, it may always not be number one or two but would be certainly at higher level than the earlier status. More you give, more will come to you. More you love and respect others, others will give you back more than you gave. Doing good to others is also winning.

Yes, it is possible for you too; you just need to believe yourself. So, what do you want to be ?

A सिकन्दर or a soldier of a team ?

I am sure you would like to be a hero, the Sikandar.

Hold on to your answer and start marching accordingly!

Key Take Away:

The world is really yours, but you need to strongly desire and work hard.

A good quote to remember by great APJ Abdul Kalam

'Dreams are not those which you see in your sleep, but are those, which don't allow you to sleep.'

While writing this book, I also didn't have proper sleep for several days, since I wanted to share my 45 years of experience with my countrymen with a hope to contribute a little from my side; and it was not so easy as I thought. So, though thinking is must, planning and implementation takes time and requires lot of patience and courage, if implementing in an adverse environment!

Thanks to my parents, wife, gurus and well-wishers across the country!

But this is not end of my journey ...
I still want to improve and progress.

Your Notes/What do I need to clarify from the Author

May please approach the author at:
sapan_bardhan@rediffmail.com

Polycab India Limited

(Connecting with aspirations)

Ajay T Jaisinghani & Ramesh T Jaisinghani

- Whole - Time Directors

Polycab's eyes are firmly fixed on the future. Looking ahead, we see an era where only the agile, the game changers and the quick learners will thrive. With this in mind, we continue to pursue an aggressive growth plan, focusing on predicting consumer behaviour, shaping the future of customer experience, and optimising our production processes for high quality, highly customised and on-time delivery.

Ever since inception five decades ago, fulfilling the dreams of customers and society has been one of our core objectives. We make a difference through the products we offer, the innovation that we unveil, the wide network of business partners and internal talent pool that we nurture, the quality standards that we adhere to, and the care that we extend to the community.

We are crafting a new transformation roadmap with zest and are poised for a grand leap into the next growth trajectory. In the last few years the Polycab management has been broadening its horizons with the introduction of Fast Moving Electrical Goods (FMEG) with an aim to become a complete electrical products solution provider. This move is already paying dividends. Polycab as of today is a name to reckon with in the Fans, LED, Switches and Switchgear segments. More recent forays into appliances like Geysers and like electric irons have met with an enthusiastic response.

Going forward, we will continue to innovate around customer aspirations and grow our leadership position across product categories. We will continue to stay grounded in our core values of simplicity, teamwork, trust-building, customer focus, and fulfilling commitments of our different stakeholders.

Polycab India Ltd, today is the largest manufacturer in the wires and cables industry in India in terms of volume, product variety, and largest distribution network. Underpinning our leadership position are our solid business fundamentals, which include multi-location manufacturing with a high degree of backward integration, a comprehensive product portfolio, strong brand positioning, robust distribution network, and experienced management.

We provide one of the most extensive range of products like Power Cables, Control Cables, Instrumentation Cables, Solar Cables, Building Wires, Flexible Cables, Flexible/ Single Multi-core Cables, Communication Cables and others including Welding Cables, Submersible Flat and Round Cables, Rubber Cables, Overhead Conductors, Railway Signalling Cables, Specialty Cables and Green Wires.

Apart from a stellar lineup of wires and cables, we have made inroads into the highly competitive FMEG market, with products like fans, LED lighting and luminaires, switches and switchgears, home appliances, solar products and conduits and accessories.

In 2009, the company diversified into the engineering procurement and construction ('EPC') business which includes the design, engineering, supply execution and commissioning of power distribution and rural electrification projects.

The Company strives to deliver customized and innovative products with world class quality and service. Most of our manufacturing facilities are accredited with quality with **ISO 9001, ISO 14001** and **ISO 45001**. The Company's Central Quality Test Laboratory at Halol is accredited by **NABL** and approved by **Underwriters Laboratories (UL)**. Certain products are also in compliance to various National and International Quality Standards like **Bureau of Indian Standards (BIS), British Approval Service for Electrical Cables (BASEC), UL and International Electrotechnical Commission (IEC).**

In addition to ensure quality products and in our continual improvement journey, we adopted Employee Engagement practices like 5S (Work Place Management), Autonomous Maintenance (Jishu Hozen ... one of 8 TPM pillars) - aiming at zero breakdown of machines are also in place. Our endeavour for a quality product and experience to the end users have enabled us to manufacture Cables and Wires with almost nil defect.

One of the key aspects of our quick success is that we are a People -Focussed company. Since inception of the company we have ensured to see a complete happy end-to-end environment in the overall process of product manufacturing and customer experience. The whole ecosystem should be happy which includes employees, suppliers, service partners etc which in turn make our customers happy, and The supplier – customer concept of **Total Quality Management (TQM)**. We encourage employees to come with new ideas, promote **Kaizen Philosophy** and are always accessible to them. We at

Polycab give topmost priority to SAFETY. All our dashboards and meetings start with incident statistics.

Another important part of our overall business process is Training. We have training modules and process in place by which employees are able to upgrade their knowledge on the Technical Processes and Latest Standards of the World, Technical Knowhow, Management Systems etc., and of course the Critical Success factors.

The Company's unwavering commitment to quality and customer delight has fuelled its rise from being India's largest wire and cable manufacturer to becoming the country's leading end-to-end electrical solutions brand. As of today, the Company offers contemporary, high-quality products across diverse categories and for every need.

Going forward, we will continue to innovate around customer aspirations and grow our leadership position across product categories. We will continue to stay grounded in our core values of simplicity, teamwork, trust-building, customer focus, and fulfilling commitments of our different stakeholders

In our journey to become India's most preferred end-to-end electrical solutions brand, we seek your continued commitment and support.

Address: 'Polycab House', Pandit Satwalekar Marg,
Mahim (west), Mumbai
Tel: 022 – 24327074/67351400

Success Journey of Lean Manufacturing at MSME Clusters, Aurangabad!

Rajendra Potdar
CEO, MABEC

In November' 2016, I received an invitation from Quality council of India to participate in the Bid opening process for Selection of Registered Lean Management Consultants (LMCs) under Lean Competitive scheme by MSME, Govt of India. We had submitted bid documents for two Lean Clusters at Aurangabad, formed under the Lean competitive scheme. Both the clusters were formed with the initiative of Greaves Cotton Ltd. There were 6 Units in One cluster and 7 units in second cluster. My colleagues Mr Bardhan, Mr Roy and Myself were very keen to help the MSME sector after supporting many Large companies for more than three decades in Manufacturing Excellence (Lean and TPM).

Except us, all other organisations had a Lean Cluster experience. Quality Council of India was coordinating for the bidding process. Mr Rastogi represented QCI and Mr Daptardar Abhay, Asst. Director MSME DI, Mumbai was responsible to ensure a fair and transparent bidding process.

Our Road Map had an Implementation period of 18 months divided into 5 Milestones ... Diagnostic Study Report (DSR), Developing and Implementation of Milestone Based Improvement Projects (MBIPs), Training on the concepts of Lean and associated Tools & Techniques, Verifying Stage wise Progress and Submitting Final Report.

After the presentation, a lot of queries were raised by cluster members. One key question asked by members of both the clusters was, whether we will be able to complete the assignment as we did not have any experience in MSME . We assured them that though we did not have experience in MSME, our team was extremely passionate to help them. Further our rich experience of Lean/TPM implementation at Large corporates/ Industries would be very useful to execute the assignment successfully.

Finally QCI announced results of selection of LMCs for both the clusters. Much to our surprise MABEC got selected as Lean Manufacturing Consultants to two clusters at Aurangabad! GCCE 1 and GCCE 2 Aurangabad Engine Clusters. Mr Roy S N and Mr Sapan Bardhan were Lean Consultants for these clusters. We were extremely delighted with the results and thanked QCI, MSME and Cluster Units for showing trust in us.

Now the challenge was to begin the Journey of Phase1 Preparation of Diagnostic Study Report. With great enthusiasm we started the Lean journey in these two clusters. Initially in Jan'2017 Mr Bardhan, Mr Roy and I took Photographs and videos of all the units for recording opportunities for improvements. We started with a bang! There was mixed response from the Units. We had circulated format for Base line data collection by each unit in advance. Required data was for Labour productivity, Capital Productivity, Annual Savings, Quality Performance, Inventory turns, Number of Kaizen, Recognition Certificates, HR Training hours, Lead Time, Cycle Time, Value added ratio, On time delivery, Throughput delivery, Equipment Availability, OEE and Floor space freed etc.

In the month of March'2017, we held kick-off meeting of all the owners, Lean Coordinators, Greaves Purchase Team to clarify the roles of all the stake holders. We started with a hope to transform each member of unit in the cluster with cooperation of owners and all employees. Every one took oath and promised to cooperate with the consultants for their own benefits. After this meet our relations strengthened further. It was a big challenge, initially DSR Phase got delayed by 6 months as data and information was not available. We overcame these initial hurdles and completed Phase 1 audit by QCI and MSME successfully.

Phase 2 onwards we started training cluster units regularly on Lean Tools and Techniques such as 5S, SOPs, VSM, Visual Control, Kaizen ... blitz of rapid improvement process, TPM, SMEDs/Quick Changeover, JIT, KANBAN, Pokayoke, Cellular Layout etc.... depending upon their applicability. Every unit took eight to ten different lean projects. We had a Gemba approach in the implementation of Lean Journey. In all the remaining three phases our momentum was good.

Hats off to Mr Bardhan and Mr Roy for showing the highest level of commitment. They became a Coach, a Teacher and a Friend of the employees. Sometimes they became very tough as a task master to get desired results. In the latter half of phases of the cluster we got very good response from all the units as they understood the importance of the Lean journey for their own survival. QCI, MSME conducted remaining three Miles stone based Audits and we were successful in each of the phases with appreciation from Auditors.

Final Phase, MBR 5 stage Audit took place from 16th to 19th March'2019 jointly by QCI and MSME. On 20th

March'2019, the closing meeting took place at Greaves Cotton, Chikalthana Factory, Aurangabad. Based on the auditors feedback and witnessing Lean Implementation status /progress in different plants. Mr Abhay Daptardar, Asst Director MSME DI Mumbai congratulated all the units of both clusters for clearing 5th and final Phase audit successfully.

He also declared that both the clusters fall in top Five Successful clusters of Maharashtra. In his closing remarks Mr Daptardar mentioned that this was one of the best audit he has seen with the highest level of worker engagement on the shop floor . He asked the audience to applaud for MABEC team! It was like a dream come true for all of us!

Experience of associating with learned auditors like Mr Shastry, Mr Vishwas Badkas, Mr Rohit Tyagi and Mr Abhay Daptardar was great. Overall we had a wonderful Learning experience.

Following are the Major Tangible Benefits (with approx. percentages) obtained:

- Quality Defects PPM - 50% reduction
- Space reclaimed for productive work - 10 to 15%
- Increase in Inventory Turnover - 10 to 20%
- Reduction in Manufacturing Lead Time - 5 to 30%
- Improvement in OEE (Model Machines) - 10 to 15%
- No. of Kaizens generated across different Lean clusters - >1100
- Increase in productivity - 8 to 20%
- Savings - Rs. 270 Lakhs approx. (both clusters)

- Establishing Good Management Systems/Practices involving Total Workforce and thus creating an environment of Safety, High Morale & Quality Consciousness.

Abraham Lincoln used to say *"I do the very best I know how, the very best I can, and I mean to keep on doing so until the end".*

Above quote talks about the consistency of doing good work. We are what we repeatedly do, Excellence, and then is not an act but a Habit.

Today, we are proud that we showed a Lean excellence path to thirteen units of two clusters for their own Growth, Continual Improvement, Sustenance and Survival!

To conclude, this Lean Journey helped us achieve our main purpose of creating value for our MSME Cluster units and society at large.

Contact: rajendra@mabec.in M: 9819599768

Your Notes/What do I need to clarify from the Author

May please approach the author at:
sapan_bardhan@rediffmail.com

Swami Vivekananda's Message to the Youth

- Swami Satyadevananda
Secretary - Ramakrishna Mission, Mumbai

Swami Vivekananda epitomizes a very high form of an Ideal to be sought to achieve in life.

It put forth such a high standard of achievement in life that only a very daring and courageous man can aspire to emulate it. No doubt that even a failure on to this path will stand head and shoulder above the successes of the most men of ordinary rung. It is because of the very intrinsic character of the Ideal it places before us to follow. Therefore, it is not very strange that only young hearts alone get attracted to it as the young ones have that optimism, idealism, courage and will to dream and deliver.

If this ideal has to be adopted, youth is the time; or have that Will to deliver what it demands.

To such hearts on fire, a few bullet points can be made of Swami Vivekananda's message.

1. Believe in yourself.
2. Don't take it for granted because it's said by someone or mentioned in a book, verify.
3. Stand up and keep doing and do not stop, till the goal is reached.
4. Take responsibility on your own shoulders.
5. Stop crying and complaining and find out the solution to the problem
6. Believe in the power of goodness, righteousness Truth.
7. Not jealousy but co-operation

8. Unselfishness, live for others, live for an Ideal
9. Lead by serving
10. Seeking Knowledge, not pleasure should be the purpose of our actions.

These ideas, values and principles will not only be helpful for any person to scale Mount Everest of achievement in any field or walk of life, but it will also make him the icon of character, setting new standards and bars for others to follow, motivate and inspire.

If you read the works of Swami Vivekananda you will get an opportunity to study these ideas in depth. Alternatively, you can interact with the great achievers who have followed these ideas in their life. You can also visit any branches of Ramakrishna Math and Ramakrishna Mission and avail any programs, lectures etc. on the ideas of Swami Vivekananda. Most importantly, deliberate on these ideas and run its simulations into your head again and again till these ideas flow smoothly into your veins and ultimately become part and parcel of your person, till YOU BECOME THE VERY IDEAL, YOU WERE TRYING TO FOLLOW.

I wish you all the very best in your life, career and struggle for success and glory.

Address: ***Ramakrishna Math and Ramakrishna Mission***
12th Road, Khar (W), Mumbai - 400 052
Tel No. - 6181 8000, 2646 4363
website: www.rkmkhar.org

***

Mahavir International ... a Brief Introduction

- CA Vijay Singh Bapna
Immediate Past International President – Apex

(Shri Shanti Kumar Jain, Rtd. IPS is the current International President – Apex and CA Anil Jain is the International Secretary General - Apex)

Mahavir International (M.I) is a Non-Religious Social Service Organisation and was started 45 years back on 4th July 1975 by few senior bureaucrats and businessmen in Jaipur who were social service oriented like-minded people. The idea was to have a platform through which an organization can propagate the principles of Lord Mahavir, mainly non-violence, and providing solace and relief to all living beings who cannot afford. The organization is supposed to provide help in medical, educational, child care, protection of environment and other fields of daily life.

Founders realised that most of the social service organizations were from overseas and there were hardly any good 'Make in India Service Organization' in India and keeping that in mind, Mahavir International was established without **Caste and Creed**.

The organization follows the principle of Lord Mahavir. It's an an organization committed to conversation of the glorious intellectual, cultural and moral values that have always ensured an enviable prestige for India at the global level. As Lord Mahavir used to preach 'love and serve others', our motto is "LOVE ALL SERVE ALL" and "LIVE AND LET LIVE".

Aims:

- To spread teachings of lord Mahavir all over the world.
- To follow path of truth, non-violence and love.
- Live and Let Live … Love All Serve All.
- To provide solace and relief to all living beings.
- To conserve the glorious intellectual, cultural and moral values.

Service Works:

Today we have approx. 400 centres across the country, having thousands of members including Virs and Viras (male members are called Vir and females are called Vira). We organize various types of activities to meet day to day needs of society. Many medical camps for human and animals are organized, which includes Viklang camps where we fix Callipers, give Tricycles, hearing aid etc. All members are dedicated and undertake service-oriented tasks, they take lead in organizing service projects. We have many members who give their time and money for the cause.

We also get funds from corporates, business people and others. Most of the people appreciate our work and know that the money is being used for the right purpose. The donations received in Mahavir International Foundation Trust have 80G exemption. Trust is also approved under FCRA.

At many centers, we have our own place to operate, for instance - six hospitals at Delhi, one in Faridabad, Nagaur, Dungarpur, Alwar, Nokha, Siliguri, Jaipur , Chittorgarh and Nagpur to name a few. Apart from this we have many clinics for eyes, dental and general check-ups at many other cities.

We have 7 National Projects:

- Green and Clean India
- Medical with Special Emphasis on Eye.
- Child Care and Baby Kits Distribution.
- Women Empowerment.
- Blood, Organ/ Body Donation.
- Education and Skill Development.
- Pregnancy to Infancy.
- Thalassemia Prevention.

The advent and continued working of Mahavir International is a powerful medium of social change, which emerged in response to and also as a solution to the increasing need for citizens to take concrete action for social causes. When several people take action in the same direction, their diverse backgrounds and experiences are combined and makes it possible to step out from conventional patterns of answers, to make a difference.

Contact No. (Apex office at Jaipur):
(0141) - 2612949/ 2616949; 09929853394 - Mr. Ashok
Email: office@mahavir.international

***

Your Notes/What do I need to clarify from the Author

May please approach the author at:
sapan_bardhan@rediffmail.com

Message from Prajapati Brahmakumaris Ishwariya Vishwa Vidyalaya, Mount Abu

- Dr. E V Swaminathan
B. Tech, DDH, PGDH, MSc (Psychology), MSc (Counselling), MBA, PhD

Corporate Trainer, Counsellor and Consultant with a clear focus on Value Based Society.

Om Shanti and please accept lots of greetings of peace and happiness!

It's with great pleasure, I acknowledge the words of wisdom and experience reflected in his book by Brother Sapan ji.

I am sure his insights would inspire you to reflect, explore and experiment to make our life much more meaningful.

Shri Sapan and I met for the first time in an Engineers Conference at the Brahmakumari's headquarters in Mount Abu.

It's said where physics ends, meta physics starts and that was the common thread between us.

The application of science and engineering to enhance the quality of life.

I have been associated with the Brahmakumaris Vidyalaya for the last 25 years. It has showed me a new way of life. It has helped to connect with my inner divine self and thereby associate with nature and everyone with peace, purity and unconditional love.

It has certainly given a new direction in my life. I always wanted to be a helping hand to people and thereby make this society a better place to live in.

But I never knew the path, until I realised that making people aware of their own real self and empowering them could be the best way of social service.

At present the whole world is passing through a very dark and fearful patch of life and we all are aware that after night there going to be a dawn.

I am happy to share that the Almighty God has drawn a cosmic blue print for World transformation. So it's the best time and opportunity to connect with the self and the Almighty God and become an instrument for change.

I request all of you to learn the technique of Rajayoga Meditation taught in the Brahmakumari's Vidyalaya free of cost.

Let us all join together and make this world healthy and happy.

With lots of love ~

Highlights of Dr. Swaminathan:

- *Conducted sessions in countries of Asia, Africa and Middle East.*
- *Has an unique distinction of conducting Training at the highest battle field of the world at SBS (Siachen Battle School) at India - Pakistan - China border.*
- *He has also appeared on numerous television talk shows which are being aired on 'Peace of Mind' TV and 'Awakening TV'.*
- *He has trained students at IITs at Kharagpur, Mumbai, Kanpur and Centre of Excellence – IIMs at Calicut, Lucknow, Amritsar, JNU and NIFT at New Delhi*
- *Research Guide in Emotional and Quantum Intelligence*

Contact: Ph: 9082263982; E-mail: evswami@gmail.com

***

Sri Aurobindo International Centre of Education, Pondicherry

(Compilation from on-line literatures on Sri Aurobindo Ashram)

Sri Aurobindo International Centre of Education, an integral part of **Sri Aurobindo Ashram**, serves as a field for experiment and research in education. Sri Aurobindo considered the formation of a new system of education as one of the best means of preparing the future humanity to manifest upon earth a divine consciousness and a divine life. In a convention held at Pondicherry in 1951, it was resolved to establish an International University Centre in the town as a fitting memorial to Sri Aurobindo and accordingly Sri Aurobindo International University Centre was inaugurated by the Mother on 6th January, 1952. In 1959, the Mother decided to rename it the Sri Aurobindo International Centre of Education.

The Centre of Education provides education from Kindergarten to the College levels of study. Its subjects include Humanities, Sciences, Languages, Engineering Technology, Physical Education and has facilities for learning drawing, painting, handwork, music and dancing - Indian and Western - dramas and arts and crafts. In addition to several libraries and laboratories, there are also opportunities for practical and manual work. It aspires to represent the cultures of different regions of the world, with the idea that every nation should make a unique contribution to a cultural synthesis and promoting mutual understanding and humanity.

The primary aim of this institution is to allow young souls

to grow into a higher life through a comprehensive, integral education. It is the teacher's task to create for every student the necessary conditions for his development and to awaken in him the joy of learning and discovery. Instead of filling the students with mere book knowledge, they should be encouraged to develop the gift of intuition which every child naturally possesses until it loses it through wrong education and teaching. Moreover, the emphasis is to be on integral education: the Mother made it clear that she did not want pale and weak pupils. Therefore, the daily sports program in the evening is compulsory for all students.

The main emphasis in the lessons should not be on factual knowledge, but on the growth of consciousness and the capacity for autonomous self-development. The Mother's specific call to the teachers was -

'We are here to open the way of the Future to children who belong to the Future'

The Centre is an experiment in the process of growth, a very comprehensive and radical experiment which may still need decades to reach its full potential. The Mother had very high expectations of this institution.

If we want this education to have its maximum result, it should begin even before birth; in this case it is the mother herself to proceed with this education by means of a twofold action: first - upon herself for her own improvement and second - upon the child whom she is forming physically. For it is certain that the nature of the child to be born depends very much upon the mother who forms it, upon her aspiration and will as well as upon the material surroundings in which she lives. To see that her thoughts are always beautiful and pure, her feelings always noble and fine, her material surroundings as harmonious as possible and full of a great simplicity. Even if she has a conscious and definite will to form the child according to the highest ideal she can conceive, then the very best conditions will be realised so that the child can come into the world with his/her utmost potentialities.

There are parents who know their children must be educated and who try to do what they can. But very few, even among those who are most serious and sincere, know that the first thing to do, in order to be able to educate a child, is to educate oneself, to become conscious and master of oneself so that one never sets a bad example to one's child. For it is above all through example that education becomes effective. To speak good words and to give wise advice to a child has very little effect if one does not oneself give him an example of what one teaches. Sincerity, honesty, straightforwardness, courage, disinterestedness, unselfishness, patience, endurance, perseverance, peace, calm, self-control are all things that are taught infinitely better by example than by beautiful speeches. Parents have a high ideal and always act in accordance with it and you will see that little by little your child will reflect this ideal in himself and spontaneously manifest the qualities you would like to see expressed in his nature. Quite naturally a child has respect and admiration for his parents, unless they are quite unworthy, they will always appear to their child as demi-gods whom he will try to imitate as best he can.

Parents are to be aware of the disastrous influence of their own defects, impulses, weaknesses and lack of self-control have on their children. If wish to be respected by a child have respect for yourself and be worthy of respect at every moment. Never be authoritarian, despotic, impatient or ill-tempered. When your child asks you a question, do not give him a stupid or silly answer under the pretext that he cannot understand you. You can always make yourself understood if you take enough trouble; and in spite of the popular saying that it is not always good to tell the truth, it is always good to tell the truth but that the art consists in telling it in such a way as to make it accessible to the mind of the hearer. In early life, until he is twelve or fourteen, the child's mind is hardly open to abstract notions and general ideas. And yet you can train it to understand these things by using concrete images, symbols or parables. Up to quite an advanced age and for some who mentally always remain children, a narrative, a story, a tale well told teaches much more than any number of theoretical explanations.

Do not scold your child without good reason and only when it is quite indispensable. A child who is too often scolded gets hardened to rebuke and no longer attaches much importance to words or severity of tone. And above all, take good care never to scold him for a fault which you yourself commit. Children are very keen and clear-sighted observers; they soon find out your weaknesses and note them without pity.

When a child has done something wrong, see that he confesses it to you spontaneously and frankly; and when he has confessed, with kindness and affection make him understand what was wrong in his movement so that he will not repeat it, but never scold him, a fault confessed must always be forgiven. You should not allow any fear to come between you and your child, fear is a pernicious means of education - it invariably gives birth to deceit and lying. Only a discerning affection that is firm yet gentle and an adequate practical knowledge will create the bonds of trust that are indispensable for you to be able to educate your child effectively. And do not forget that you have to control yourself constantly in order to be equal to your task and truly fulfil the duty which you owe your child by the mere fact of having brought him into the world.

Focus in this Centre is on **Integral Education** which consists of education on Physical, Vital, Mental, Psychic and Spiritual and to continue till end of the existing life.

Qualities of a Successful Teacher ~

1. Completely self-controlled, not only showing anger but also to remain undisturbed & quite, under all circumstances.
2. Self-confident but to be aware that he also needs to continually progress on what he knows.
3. Not having any sense of superiority over his students, nor preferential treatment to anybody.
4. Quite aware of that all are equal spiritually and have a global understanding.

According to Sri Aurobindo - the teacher and the parent is to help a child to educate himself, to develop his own intellectual, moral, aesthetic and practical competencies and grow freely, rather than pressurising and kneading him.

Address: No. 9, Marine Street, White Town,
Puducherry – 605002
Tel: 0413 – 2233666
E-mail: manojdg@sriaurobindoashram.org

***

Your Notes/What do I need to clarify from the Author

May please approach the author at:
sapan_bardhan@rediffmail.com

Acknowledgements

Dignitaries who responded well to our survey on 'SUCCESS Exercise' (prioritizing the parameters of success, what success means to them etc.) are:

1.	Dr. Pratap Dighavkar, IPS	Special Inspector General of Police (P.C.W.C), Maharashtra
2.	Dr. Sudhakar Shinde, IRS	CEO, Ayushman Bharat, Maharashtra
3.	Sri Rajesh Kumar Arnold, IES	Ex TRAI Board Member
4.	Dr. (Mrs.) Rama A Bhoslae	Principal, Govt. College of Education, Panvel, Navi Mumbai
5.	Dr. (Mrs.) Lakshmi Mohan	Director - ITM Business School, Navi Mumbai
6.	Ms Priya Sreedharan	Film Producer - Open Air Films
7.	Sri Vijay Singh Bapna	International President, Mahavir International (2015-19)
8.	Sri Sudesh Bhosle	Playback Singer, Mimicry & Voice Dubbing Artist
9.	Dr. Indrajit Bhattacharya	Director, NABET (National Accreditation Board for Education & Training) Govt. of India
10.	Sri Ramesh T Jaisinghani	Director, Polycab India Ltd.

11.	Sri Abhay Daptardar	Astt. Director, Ministry of MSME, Govt. of India
12.	Dr. Radhakrishnan Pillai	Best Seller Author Deputy Director, CIILS, University of Mumbai
13.	Sri Sudhir Kalokhe	President, Quality Circle Forum of India
14.	Dr. Girish Gune	Proprietor Gune Hospital, Panvel, Maharashtra
15.	Sri K B Bharati	Director, QCFI and Chairman, Mumbai Chapter
16.	Sri Arvind Bodhankar	Jt. Executive President & Chief Sustainability Officer, UltraTech Cement
17.	Sri Chandrasekhar Ponnuswamy	Founder Director Practus Business Transformation Pvt. Ltd.
18.	Sri Rajendra Potdar	CEO & Founder, MABEC
19.	Sri Venkateshwar Pandey	Sr. VP (Refractory), JSW Steel, Dolvi, MS
20.	Sri Pradip Patra	Rtd. Sr. VP JSW Steel Dolvi, MS
21.	Sri Dilip Jha	Sr. General Manager (Operations), Emami Group
22.	Sri Bibhasendra Sen	Director, Capital Markets Northern Arc Capital
23.	Sri Dnyanesh Kabra	Director, Kabra Group, Waluj, Aurangabad
24.	Sri Manish Bothara	Director, Jinendra Industries, Chikalthana, Aurangabad

25.	Sri Amol Kadam	Director, Suraj Tools, Chikalthana, Aurangabad
26.	Sri Vijay S Kanugo	CEO, Jat Metals, Waluj, Aurangabad
27.	Sri D K Srivastava	Executive Director, Quality Circle Forum of India
28.	Sri P S Ghose	President & Chief – Projects, Kalyani Steels Ltd.
29.	Sri Sarvesh Dubey	Associate Vice President (Operations), RSPL Ltd.
30.	Sri Srikrishna Patankar	Rtd. Addl. Chief Engineer, Industrial Engg. RCF Ltd. Trombay Unit
31.	Dr. Vivek Yakkundi	Professor & Dean Lokmanya Tilak College of Engineering Koparkhairne, Navi Mumbai
32.	Sri Rajesh Mishra	General Manager, Supplier QA Greaves Cotton Ltd.
33.	Sri Vivek Shinde	Retailer, Shilpa Medicals & a Social Worker
34.	Sri M G Arun	Chief Editor, India Today
35.	Sri Rohit Tyagi	Lean Consultant, QCI
36.	Sri Vishwas Badkas	Independent Consultant
37.	Sri Anand Rao	Sr. Vice President, HR Adani Power (Thermal Division)

38.	Sri Ajay Agarwal	Product Appl. Specialist Auto & Truck OEM and Fleets Asia Pacific, Shell Global Solutions
39.	Sri Anurag Rastogi	Joint Director, NABET, Quality Council of India
40.	Sri Tukaram Kandakure	CEO, Dhananjay Group, Aurangabad
41.	Sri Yashpal Singh	Dy. GM/Head – Corporate Safety, Godrej
42.	Sri Suresh Kumar	Executive President & Chief HR Officer, Polycab India Ltd.
43.	Sri Ganesh Deshmukh	Municipal Commissioner, Panvel
44.	Sri Mangesh Parulekar	Owner, Orion Mall, Panvel
45.	Sri Ashish Gupta	Head - Opr. Excellence Academy GM – Corporate HR (L & D) Tata Motors Ltd.
46.	Sri P R Dighavkar	Ex. Indian Air Force Executive
47.	Dr. Nitin Mhatre	Consultant Orthopaedic Surgeon, Mhatre Accident Hospitals, Panvel
48.	Dr Santosh K. Nair	Director, Nair Super Speciality, Eye Hospital, New Panvel
49.	Dr. Nitin Powale	N Connect Homeopathy Clinic, Panvel - New Panvel
50.	Siraz Henry	Film Producer & Writer

References:

Literatures/Periodic Magazines/Messages of:

1. Sri Aurobindo Ashram
2. Ramakrishna Mission
3. Bramha Kumaris
4. Mahavir International
5. TQM, TPM, Lean Manufacturing
6. Management Seminars
7. Linked In
8. You Tube Videos on Management
9. Talks of Management Professionals

Your Notes/What do I need to clarify from the Author

May please approach the author at:
sapan_bardhan@rediffmail.com

Sapan Bardhan

... a Game Changer for Individuals & Organisations !

(Brief Profile)

Sapan Bardhan is a:

Motivational Speaker

People & Organisation Development Coach

Lean Consultant

Author of book 'Unfolding Success ~ New Era – New Approach'

Sapan's Client List includes ~

MTI – SAIL, Ranchi; Hindustan Lever; Bhushan Steel; UL DQS (India); Poshs Metal; BALCO; Tata BlueScope Steel; Ordnance Factory, Progeon (Infosys), Emami Group, Ultra Tech (Aditya Birla Group), Ruchi Soya; Polycab; Relaxo Footwear etc. are the organisations where he supported through various HR, Safety, Environment & Quality System interventions.

He also supported one of the MSME clusters at Aurangabad as a lean consultant.

Sapan is one of few - who has hands on experience of execution & facilitating improvement initiatives in many organizations, training thousands of personnel through in-house & open house programs and conducting third party audits of many organizations within & outside the country. Assessed few organizations for RBNQA and many reputed organizations on the basis of their own Business Excellence Models and thus sparked minor, small, medium & large scale business organizations, having various types & nature of processes ...

to move towards continual improvement.

He has been successfully trained on TQM at USA from IRD Inc. and also on "Production efficiency for India" at Japan through AOTS.

Sapan has about thirty years of specific experience in the field of Organization Development through People Involvement & Engagement with about forty five years of overall experience.

He served Bhilai Steel Plant, an unit of SAIL dedicatedly in TQM Secretariat for three years and later a large sector steel industry for eight years and left while working in the capacity of VP (TQM & HR). He was also associated with UL DQS (India), as a lead assessor for QMS and a Trainer.

Sapan presented papers in various forums like WCTQ at Delhi, ICSQCC at Lucknow, Winners Forum at Mumbai, ICQCC at Philippines and NCQC at Hyderabad and also at ASQ, Ahm'bad in Nov'14 and was a Moderator of Panel Discussions on:

'Zero Defect – Zero Effect' at ICTQM organized by QCFI, Mumbai in Nov'2015.

'Business Excellence in Turbulent Times' by ITM & QCFI, Mumbai in Feb'2017.

His following articles have been published by ASQ in Nov'2014 and Nov'2016:

- 'Quality Excellence through Daily Work Management & Management Reviews'
- 'Mission Eklavya - People Transformation through Education & Training'.

It was indeed a prestigious landmark when Sapan led the Indian Delegation to Manila, during International Convention for ICQCC in 1999.

He introduced 'Learning Management Concept' - a departure from traditional training, by his own developed Module 'Mission Eklavya'.

Sapan's concern for people satisfaction & Unique People Management style made him an acknowledged leader in his areas of operations.

His recent successful motivational programs were at -
Mgmt. Institute of Technology – Aurangabad (MS);
Monnet Steel - Raigarh (Chhattisgarh);
Everest Industries – Nashik (MS);
Ultratech Cement – Ratnagiri, (MS)
Govt. College of Education – Panvel (MS).

His interactive way of training people with down to earth practical examples and above all his sincere approach in convincing the participants, made him a very popular choice as a faculty & a coach.

His overall Success may be rated between 90% - 95%.

Socially/Spiritually Sapan Bardhan is also well connected with Ramakrishna Mission, Sri Aurobindo Ashram, Brahmakumaris & Mahavir International.

He may be reached through:
sapan_bardhan@rediffmail.com

***

Suggested Further Readings

All books, articles, messages issued by responsible organisations committed to betterment of society are useful.

List of Training and Workshop Modules

1. Developing a Super Motivated Team in New Normal
2. Unfolding Success
3. Mission Possible
4. Applying Manufacturing Cost Reduction Levers
   ~ Survival of the Fittest
5. Boosting Productivity through
   ~ Eradication of Non-Value Activities
6. Empowering thru Digital Technology Convergence
7. Employee Safety & Wellbeing in the Post Pandemic Era
8. 'Mission Eklavya'
   ~ the Risk Based Identification of Training needs
9. Zero Defect Zero Effect
10. Leadership Excellence/Effective Manager
11. Realizing Vision & Mission
12. Lean Manufacturing
13. Problem Solving Approaches
14. 5S - Work Place Management
15. Total Productive Maintenance (TPM)
16. Autonomous Maintenance (Jishu Hozen)
17. Total Quality Management (TQM)
18. Effective Integrated Management Systems

You may please reach us through:
sapan_bardhan@rediffmail.com

'It is easy to defeat someone, but it is very hard to win someone'

- Dr. APJ Abdul Kalam

"Asato ma sadgamaya,
Tamso ma jyotirmaya,
Mrityoma amritam gamaye"

Compliments to the Author

I am proud to say that ***I am yet to see a better motivator than Mr. Bardhan.*** I am sure he would reap success in whatever he undertakes.

Ajay Jaisinghani
Director – Polycab India Ltd.

We always read, listen. Mind is like a parachute, it works well when it's open and ***Mr. Sapan Bardhan's simple yet enthusiastic approach works as a catalyst to open the mind.*** He can break hesitation in a person, whether he is a new age Engineer, Experienced Professional or a Seasoned Entrepreneur and make all of them participate with passion and commitment.

Rajesh Mishra
General Manager – SQA, Greaves Cotton Ltd.

Sapan Bardhan Sir has been our Lean Manufacturing Guide. He has transformed our company both physically and mindset wise. His friendly and practical style of communication keeps the workers and trainees involved. His personal anecdotes during the training programs make the learning process very humorous and enjoyable. ***This self-learning method has made the lean manufacturing journey a very happy one.***

Manish Bothara
Jinendra Industrial Co. MIDC - Chikalthana, Aurangabad

While working with Mr. Bardhan, during day to day interaction with him, we could understand the goal behind his training since ***he focusses on actual implementation rather than mere documentation.*** Surprisingly, It's worth to note that he is willing to do for the society and the nation with same positive thoughts, for development of India.

Vijay Kanugo
CEO - JAT Metal Pressing Pvt. Ltd., MIDC - Waluj, Aurangabad

He is professionally known to me for last twenty years, very knowledgeable in management systems. Mr. Bardhan is an excellent trainer for people at senior management levels. ***I have personally benefited by attending his program.*** I am sure anybody attending his program will certainly get benefitted.

S. R. Ravichandran
Ex Head - Operations & Quality Tata BlueScope Ltd.

Sapan is an excellent trainer, communicator and coach for influencing mindset towards management systems. He is very diligent, committed and believes in work ethics; it was a pleasure working with him. ***Persons attending his programs and/or working with him will really enjoy and get all answers.***

A V Shivaramakrishnan
Ex. General Manager - Assessments LRQA Ltd., South West Asia.

Sapan is a very committed person and has a rich experience in OD with focus on deliverable and execution and very passionate about getting results. ***I remember, when I witnessed him conducting Vision Workshop for Top Management having more than 75 Senior Executives of Polycab, single handed.*** I am sure, every individual attending his program will get benefits.

Suresh Kumar, Sr. Vice President -
Human Resources - Mafatlal Group

It was a very good experience for all of us at Polycab, having Mr. Sapan Baradhan associated with us. He was instrumental in developing a strong base in terms of good management systems across all units, all cadres from top to bottom. ***People Development is his focus for sustenance of all systems and achievements. He is very popular as an effective trainer & motivator.***

Ramesh Jaisinghani - Director
Polycab India Ltd.

We have received positive feedbacks to your excellent session; students were impressed with your high expertise in the subject. ***The session was very fruitful, motivating and helpful for our students, as expected.***

Principal - MIT
Aurangabad

Bardhan Sir is an industry veteran and leadership coach. I had an opportunity to work with him ***... very down to earth, passionate but also a tough task master.*** His recent launch 'Mission Possible'/'Unfolding Success' has come up very well and has a plan to conduct across the country. I wish him ... all the success.

Arvind Bodhankar
Jt. Executive President & Chief Sustainability Officer,
UltraTech Cement, Aditya Birla Group

I know Sapan Sir, since Ispat days and admire his HR, Quality and Training capabilities. ***He has excellent grip on People Management & Administrative Control... one of his missions is People Development.. Anybody working with him gets benefits for sure.***

Ajay Agarwal – Product Application Specialist
Auto, Truck OEM and Fleets Asia Pacific,
Shell Global Solutions

Long Term Service Association Award is presented to Mr. Sapan Kumar Bardhan, ***in recognition of his association with us and as a mark of Appreciation and Goodwill.***

Dr. K Murugan
Managing Director & CEO
UL DQS India

Mr Bardhan guided us in people development under 'E&T Pillar of TPM'. ***His friendly and mentoring approach motivates the people to learn and enhance their functional skill as well as to think beyond their functional boundary, which creates positive vibes throughout the plant.***

He also gave us Risk Based Process approach based on FMEA model which helped in analysing processes, mapping the associated risks and then finding the skill gaps in people to plan the training program accordingly. ***It has also helped us in sustaining our excellence journey in productivity as well as quality.***

Dilip Kumar Jha
General Manger (Operations)
Emami Ltd.

Sapan can execute any tough assignment on the shop floor successfully. He commands respect and has sacrificing attitude towards fellow workmen.

Ramesh Vishwakarma
Executive Vice-President
Polycab India